# Write Whatever the Hell You Want

## Finding Joy and Purpose in Writing

# Nikki Hanna

*Published by Patina Publishing*
*Tulsa, Oklahoma 74120*

*neqhanna@sbcglobal.net*
*www.nikkihanna.com*

*IBSN: 978-0-9978141-4-9*

*Manufactured in The United States of America*

*Photography: Steven Michaels, Tulsa, Oklahoma*

*Cover Design: L1graphics*

*Cover Artwork: "Audacious"*
*by Nan McDowell, Jenks, Oklahoma*

*Contributors: Lhonda Harris, Tom Bush,*
*Donna Parsons, William Bernhardt, Susan Kay,*
*Melanie Corbin, Gay Martin, Cynthia Vanderpool*

# Dedication

To the little people:

**Thing I and Thing II:**
Cole Zane - My Sidekick
Bethany Kay - My Girlfriend

and

**The Sparkles:**
McCartney Page
Ellery Michelle


Be brave, you lovely little creatures. Have moxie, be bold, be audacious, be nice, and don't swear like your grandma. GoGo is not always a good role model.

When times get tough, always remember: "You're braver than you believe, stronger than you seem, and smarter than you think."—Christopher Robin

*Joyful writers don't write to get rich, although they may dream about that and even aspire to it. They write because they love to create. They relish seeing what they write blossom into a beautiful composition to be shared. It's not about the money. It's not about the fame. It's about why they write—the creation, the artistry, the sharing. Be that writer.*

# TABLE OF CONTENTS

## SECTION II
## The Craft of Writing

––––––––––––––––––––

## SECTION III
## Memoir and Contests—Paths to Joy and Purpose

---

## Section IV
## Printing/Publishing/Marketing

---

## Section V
### A Personal Path

---

## APPENDIX

# Introduction

I look back at what I knew when I started writing and realize it was precious little. Retiring from a robust career, I naively thought all that was necessary to be a writer was to start writing. That's a far stretch from reality—if a person wants to be good at it. Ten years and many learning experiences and published books later, I teach writing and have won numerous writing awards. The path to this point gives me a sense of what new writers need to do to develop into good writers.

Like me when I started, most novice writers are not aware they need to do anything. They are so wrong. Agents, editors, publishers, and seasoned writers recognize their newbie status within the first couple of paragraphs, if not in the first sentence. Readers also notice amateur writing. They might not understand why, but they know it's not up to standard.

When I coach new writers, they learn what they don't know after receiving red marks all over a copy of their first chapter. My goal is to cram as much writing craft into their heads as quickly as possible, and I don't hold back. From one session, they learn a host of principles and tedious nuances that set a writer apart. Once they learn about them in the first chapter and apply them to the rest, progress is so significant they are inspired to embrace more learning.

The key to my success is continuous learning. Per Maya Angelou's advice, "When you get give. When you learn teach," I teach writing workshops. And I wrote a book about writing, *Capture Life—Write a Memoir*, which is lush with writing techniques and elements of craft. It also explores printing, publishing, and marketing. Since the title and much of the content is focused on memoir, it was not noticed by writers of other genres—thus this book, which is broader and more robust. It, and my book, *Listen Up, Writer —How Not to Write Like an Amateur,* are designed to thrust both novice and seasoned writers of any genre into a more professional writing mode. Writers learn how to write well.

The most profound lessons learned from my writing experiences were not about writing. I learned about reality, failure, and the emotional influences writing provokes. I learned about the variety of pathways to achievement and fulfillment through writing. I learned my books have a purpose beyond their value in the marketplace. I learned there is so much more to writing books than selling them and making money. I learned why I write. And I learned how to find joy and purpose through writing.

Most writers fail to realize there are many paths to success. When I abandoned the common industry definition of success, which is selling lots of books, making lots of money, and becoming famous, I became a raging success. The following chapters reveal how I did that and how readers can find a guaranteed path to accomplishment. There are many options. This book introduces the knowledge and tools required for a person to nestle into a fulfilling sweet spot in the realm of writing and publishing.

My wish for you, dear reader, is that you develop a deeper understanding of why you write, learn the principles of your craft, and appreciate their value. My wish for you is that you define success yourself rather than accepting industry standards and that you discover a niche compatible with innate talents. My wish for you is that you realize the power and magic of your words and the legacy you create by sharing them. My wish for you is that you find so much joy and purpose in writing you can hardly stand it and you write something crazy wonderful. So write, you promising, spirited, driven, wondrous writer. Write, and write well.

# SECTION I

## How to Find
## Joy and Purpose in Writing

*You will know you are doing what you were born to do when times passes and you don't realize it.*

*Chapter 1*

# The Path to Joy

*If you have young friends who aspire to become writers, the second greatest favor you can do for them is to present them with a copy of "The Elements of Style." The first greatest, of course, is to shoot them now, while they are happy.*—Dorothy Parker

I don't shoot novice writers, but when coaching them, the second favor I do for them is tell them: "After I critique your first chapter, you will have to go home and heal because I'm going to hit you with everything I've got." They do heal, because the first greatest favor I do is convince them that craft matters, and mastering it will make them happy.

I know this from personal experience. I may not be the best writer I know, but I might be the happiest. I found my sweet spot in writing when I veered from the path of the common goal of most writers, which is to sell books, make money, and become famous. All I heard from the writer community when I started writing was this fantasy, so initially I aspired to achieve it. This meant I performed many functions I didn't enjoy, and they were not working. As a result, I was a failure—a frustrated, stressed-out writer. Most of my writer friends were swimming in the same sea of discontent.

It didn't help that all I heard from my non-writer friends were ridiculous comments about Oprah discovering my book. It happened so often and grated on me so thoroughly I considered, "How hard do I slap this person?"

I eventually solved these problems—and rather splendidly, I think. The solution brought me to an unexpected level of achievement, one outside the norm. As a result, I found my joy and purpose in writing. How did I do it? The first step involved redefining success.

**WHAT YOU WANT:** Ask yourself this: Are you wanting what everyone tells you to want, or are you focused on what it is about writing that makes you joyful? Do you even know what that is? Is what you want achievable?

Most writers are unaware of the broad spectrum of writing approaches available to them. All they hear is industry rhetoric about getting an agent, a major publisher, selling books, and making money. Therefore, they don't customize their paths to fit individual talents. Writers need not abandon the industry standard of success, but by exploring other aspects of the profession, many paths to joy and purpose are revealed.

**REALITY:** If I buy a picture frame with the photo of a handsome man in it, take it home, and put it on my dresser, that doesn't mean I have a boyfriend. Let's get real and explore the reality of the writing world. Seasoned writers know making a living as a writer is a long shot. Most would settle for touching the hem of a modest seller. They know that getting an agent and a major publisher is unlikely, no matter how good they are or how hard they try.

The odds of an author making a full-time, high-paying career out of writing are long indeed. They always have been. There are many hundreds of thousands of authors publishing books each year, both traditionally and indie. Only a few thousand will earn a living.—authorearnings.com

According to R. R. Bowker, the national book registrar, over a million books are published every year, and only about 5% result in significant sales. Most of those are from established authors or famous people.

With that many books coming out yearly, a writer is competing for sales with millions of others. I put the key words "Iowa" and "Memoirs" into Amazon's search engine to locate my first memoir, *Out of Iowa—Into Oklahoma*, and 1,584 books came up. What are the odds anyone will see mine, let alone buy it?

That brings us to the next reality. Writers make only a few dollars on each book sold. Authors get about 7.5% of net sales dollars from a publisher. An agent takes about 15% of that. The average self-published book sells fewer than 250 copies. This would generate author income of about $800.

That's on a book it took a year or more to write and cost well over $800 to have edited. Eighty percent of books produced by small-to-medium-sized publishers fail to generate substantial income. A significant percentage of books published by major publishers fail as well. The book business has always held poor odds for writers. Prospects have been made worse in recent years by a decline in demand for books and an increase in writers.

These numbers explain why there are no writers at career days. That's not all. Agents accept about 1% of manuscripts submitted and many writers never find a publisher. There is good news, though. Because of self-publishing, more writers are able to be published. This doesn't mean they are making money. A writer must work hard to sell even a hundred copies to family, friends, and contacts. This is challenging because many of these folks expect the writer to give them one and half of them don't read books. Those that do read, do so only in their preferred genre. After those initial transactions, most writers experience a severe dwindling of sales. It's not as though "You build it, and they will come." It's just not.

Marketing a book requires an intense effort over many years, two of them concentrated. In spite of publisher support, the reality is that only the author can sell his book. He is "it." This is a massive endeavor. The picture of the iceberg with its small tip sticking out of the water from the mass submerged below illustrates this perfectly. The tip represents the writing, the mass below the marketing effort.

Marketing might be worthwhile if it brought results in proportion to the effort. The reality is that most books don't sell enough volume to generate even a modest income no matter what the author does. Writers who've been around awhile know this. New writers dream of the Oprah experience.

Truckers call an area in Pennsylvania "the land of low bridges." Many a rookie driver has learned about this area the hard way. It distresses me to observe rookie writers ask, "How do I get an agent?" when they haven't even finished their book. They are ripe for getting stuck under a metaphorical bridge. I'm tempted to adapt a Bruce Willis line from *Die Hard*, "Come to Momma." I want so badly to talk to them about prospects, craft, reality, perspectives, and a whole bunch of other things.

In spite of the odds, brave writers run the gauntlet of trying to get published by a major publisher. If they land one, the aftermath is taxing. Bookstore issues compound the problems. Given these factors, why would writers chase the dream of landing a major publisher and making it onto best seller lists? Because they believe it is the ultimate accomplishment—the brass ring. I suggest there are other brass rings.

**What Is Doable:** Dreams are not always doable. Someone told those awful singers in the early tryouts of American Idol they could sing. No doubt someone also told them they could do whatever they wanted to do. These contestants would have been better served if someone had told them, "Discover what you were born to do, and do that." This doesn't mean they cannot sing and enjoy it. Rather it means they are not going to make a living at it.

Not all dreams are doable. This is difficult to hear, but for some writers, defining success as selling books, making money, and becoming famous is naive idealism squared. Like in the music industry, only a few of the most talented *and luckiest* writers achieve success because of the odds. This doesn't mean every writer cannot enjoy writing. Whatever his level of talent, he can, just as anyone can enjoy singing no matter their talent. Heck, I sing, and I cannot sing.

For some writers, defining success as selling books, making money, and becoming famous is unlikely, but they can find joy through writing. Their minds, spirits, wisdom, and crazy-wonderful selves can be shared through what they create. In this scenario, writing is a gift shared rather than a money source.

What is your writing dream? Are you dreaming it because others defined it for you? Is it based on self-awareness and realistic outcomes? Define success on your own terms. Find reasons to write other than money and fame, and add them to your portfolio of aspirations.

**SUCCESS DEFINED:** There are many avenues to writing success. Develop your own personal definition of it. Don't let others define success for you. Discover what you enjoy about writing and focus on those aspects of the profession. When I defined success this way, my frustrations vanished and my world lit up:

I wrote it, I shared it, and some people enjoyed it.

That's it. That's all. With this definition, I'm successful when the words flow. I cannot fail. If I get one email that says something I wrote changed someone's life, I'm successful. And I have a file full of such emails. I am a raging success although I've not sold a lot of books. I share my work without a focus on selling it. Most writers carry books around in their trunks to sell. I carry them around to give away. If someone throws money at me, I take it, but that's not what I'm about. I love the sparkle in the eyes of a person I've handed a book. Discovering this perspective was transforming and, with it, the joy of writing blossomed. I became a writer in crescendo.

The revelation that steered me to this point was that I wasn't making a lot of money no matter what I did. So why do all the things I dreaded? Why sit at a book signing selling for eight hours only to sell five books? Why invest hours on a social media channel only to sell two books?

Nothing I did produced enough money to make a difference, so I switched gears and focused on generosity. My writing became a gift to be shared. This freed me from the disappointment of not making money and from the marketing and technology-based activities I didn't enjoy. As a result, I achieved more recognition from helping other writers through coaching, teaching, and being active in the writer community than I was ever likely to realize through book sales. And I became more prolific because I no longer wasted time on activities I didn't enjoy or wasn't good at.

With this new definition of success, I became brave about customizing my activities to my innate talents:

**Experts say: Do research, seek an agent and a publisher, and then spend a year or two focused on marketing your book.** I'm seventy-one. I started writing at sixty-three and have published seven books. If I had spent several years researching and writing my first book, a couple of years seeking an agent and publisher (if that were even possible), another eighteen months waiting for the book to come out, and a year or two marketing it, I would still be gnashing away on that first book ten years later. I'd be dead before the second one came out. So when a book is ready, I self-publish it, do a soft, two-month launch, and move on to the next book.

**Experts say: A writer must have a platform—an extensive social media following.** I'm a technological idiot. I would rather wallpaper. Enough said. I have no platform other than a website.

**Experts say: A writer must produce a cohesive portfolio of books.** I self-publish, so my books are all over the place. I have two memoirs, a book on memoir writing, a book on leadership, a book on aging, and one composed of vignettes, essays, short stories, and poetry. That book is a compilation so varied it is unlikely any publisher would touch it. They would say, "W-h-a-a-t?" Yet feedback from writer friends and readers suggests it's my best book yet. What can I say, I'm multi-faceted, or perhaps I have ADD. Whatever. If I find my lane, I'll get in it—or not.

I write whatever the hell I want and I write it whatever way I want, and I'm incredibly productive. As a result, I'm so deliciously happy I could marry myself.

**EXPANDING THE DREAM:** My way is not right for everyone. Each writer must find his own path. The intent of this book is not to discourage writers from chasing dreams of landing a major publisher, selling books, making money, becoming famous, or whatever other goal they might have. I admire those with the gumption to aspire to that. Their spunk is impressive. I applaud their drive and wish them well.

My message is this: If you are one of those writers, make certain you chose that goal because of a fire in your belly, not because that's what the industry tells you is the measure of success. Become intensely aware of your innate strengths. Know that you can chase the industry-hyped goal while embracing other writing activities that promote a sense of purpose. By designing your dream around natural abilities and according to your personal definition of success, you are postured to revel in the joy of writing.

**A FRESH PERSPECTIVE:** With my definition of success, the goal became clear: share my knowledge and creativity while I still can. This is not the appropriate goal for everyone, but it works for me at this point in my life. Let me be clear, I still dream of a huge book success. Every writer is hungry on the inside. But I don't focus on that, and—as much as I can—I avoid performing tasks that make me unhappy to chase that remote possibility. I also want to weigh less than Anderson Cooper and have the body of Catherine Zeta Jones. But I accept that's not going to happen.

If you are a frustrated writer, consider broadening your dream. Know why you write. Match your approach to writing to innate talents. Focus on those activities that are purposeful and that give you joy. Most importantly, redefine success so a sense of accomplishment and purpose is guaranteed. And know this: Steering away from the goal of selling books and making money is not giving up. It's finding your niche—your own unique path.

Let's explore writing activities that have the potential to make you happy and learn how to avoid those that don't. Some of them will surprise you.

*Chapter 2*

# Finding Joy and Purpose

*Writing a book is an adventure. To begin with, it is a toy and an amusement. Then it becomes a mistress, then it becomes a master, then it becomes a tyrant. The last phase is that just as you are about to be reconciled to your servitude, you kill the monster and fling him to the public.*—Winston Churchill

This statement alludes to the challenges of writing and to the common afflictions of those who embrace it. Writers range from hobbyists who dabble to those aspiring to attain professional status. They all face considerable frustration. To find joy and purpose, it's important a writer discover his own niche in the writing world.

Speakers at writers' conferences have had success at selling their books or they wouldn't be presenters. They talk about how they did it and dish out the requisite "how-to" advice, but they are an exceedingly small minority of the writer pool. Very few writers can approach that level of success no matter how hard they try. I'd like to hear more speakers talk about other avenues of success. I want to hear this woman speak:

A lady I sat next to at a conference boasted that she had been published in over seventy anthologies. She wasn't making money, but she was successful. I want to know how she did it. I'm betting she was the happiest person in the workshop that day. She had found her niche—her joy in writing.

Let's explore pathways to achievement beyond selling books and making money—alternate roads that promote joy and inspire a sense of purpose.

**THE FIRST STEP:** The process of creating a fabulous work that only you can make is a joyful experience, whether it turns out to be something that is shared or not. Write every day. Ramble on. Do it for a reason or for no reason. Try new things: poetry, fiction, nonfiction, essays, articles, blogs, journaling, or memoir. This could lead to a book that combines these ramblings into a "collection" of vignettes. Or not. Doesn't matter. What matters is you feeling good about writing.

The best action you can take to equip yourself to do something different with writing is learning. I've been taking college courses and going to workshops and conferences for ten years, and I have no plans to stop. Take the first step. Sign up for a class, a workshop, or a conference.

**CONTINUOUS LEARNING:** Never give in to the feeling of knowing enough. Gandhi said, "Learn as though you will live forever." Short of the actual writing experience, learning is the best forever gift you can give yourself as a writer. What you learn becomes a part of you. It is a possession no one can ever take away.

Learning is the motor that drives achievement. It is the path out of mediocrity into the world of authorship. And it is a gift you can share. I'm not a poet, but for my friends' birthdays, I write them a poem—an exceptional gift.

The best way to learn to be a writer is to write, and the best way to become a better writer is to read. I am usually reading two books at a time, one on writing and another for enjoyment. I figure when I'm ninety, I'll be a pretty good writer. In addition to enjoyment, learning has given me a sense of purpose because when I share what I learn, I give a gift others can hold forever.

**GIFTING SQUARED:** Give the gift of your wisdom, intimate feelings, lessons learned, humor, grit, and bravado. Put your work out into the world. Write memoir. Write poems or short stories for people's birthdays, anniversaries, graduations, etc. Do readings at senior centers and other gatherings. Chronicle vacations, family events, and celebrations. Put stories in sympathy cards. Produce a family newsletter. Become the family historian. Capture life stories of older people before those stories are gone forever. Collaborate with young technical geniuses to produce what you write and give them credit. Imagine a life story printed out and distributed at a person's eightieth birthday party co-authored by you and some young whippersnapper in the family—a gift extraordinaire. Now, that is being a writer, and it has nothing to do with selling books and making money.

**PUBLICATION ALTERNATIVES:** There are many ways to be a published author. Here are only a few:

**Anthologies:** Hundreds of anthologies (collections of writings by multiple writers) are published every year from universities, writing groups, organizations, and enthusiasts. They offer a lucrative avenue to publication.

**Novellas:** A cross between a short story and a novel, the novella is a hot new book category. A typical novel runs about 300 pages. A novella runs about 100 pages, which can be read in one sitting.

**Magazines/Newsletters:** Locally produced specialty magazines and newsletters are always looking for articles. They are perfect for publishing short stories, poems, articles, and essays. The odds of getting published are much higher with them than with national publications. Better yet, volunteer to write a column or to be an editor.

**Blogging:** This can be a fabulous vehicle for sharing the gift of writing. The challenge is to make blogs clever and enticing to followers. I've judged blogs in a contest and found most of them encumbered with uninteresting posts on daily living. Bloggers must develop a talent for making the ordinary extraordinary if they expect to capture a substantial number of followers. However, If they don't care about that and are blogging for the joy of it, good for them.

The challenges of blogging are reflected in the fact that more inactive blogs exist on the Internet than active ones. People abandon them because of the required commitment to post regularly and the challenge of developing a following. The demands of blogging, if done right, may leave little time for other writing activities. Also, anything blogged is generally considered published, which can disqualify posts for other opportunities. Still, blogging offers an exceptional opportunity for a writer to share his art.

**THE WRITING COMMUNITY:** Following are ways to enjoy being a writer other than publication. They involve becoming part of the writing community. Make it your tribe.

**Writers' Groups:** Become active in a writers' group. Volunteer for projects or become an officer. I don't enjoy book signings, but I do them occasionally because my writers' group colleagues are there, and I love the camaraderie of being part of a tribe of writers.

**Teaching/Coaching:** As you become the expert described in the next chapter, consider sharing that knowledge through books, blogs, and workshops. Mentor new writers and save them some of the hardships you experienced.

**Writers' Colonies:** Find a place to write—a retreat of sorts. I go to The Writers' Colony in Eureka Springs, Arkansas, (writerscolony.org) two or three times a year. An online search will reveal such places in your area. Most retreats provide writer workshops, residency scholarships, and opportunities to commune with writers.

**Writers' Conferences:** Attend writers' conferences. They offer a tsunami of learning, thrust writers into the world of writing experts, and provide a way to commune with other writers. In addition, conferences provide an opportunity to travel to wonderful places with great hotel rates. I spent a week in New York City at a nice hotel two blocks from Times Square for $116 a night. Thousands of writers attended. It was a conference on steroids and one of the best vacations I've ever had. I had my picture taken with The Naked Cowboy in Times Square, texted it to my children with the message "I L-o-v-e New York" and to my girlfriends with the message "Eat Your Hearts Out." I often attend The University of Iowa's Writers' Festival. This is one of the best and most intense workshops in the world. It's like a mini college course. I've bonded with other writers there.

**Community Involvement:** Support local bookstores, libraries, and writers' events. Participate in book clubs and go to readings of other authors. With community involvement, your reputation as an author will flourish and you will become a part of something bigger than yourself.

**Reviews:** Support other writers. Read their books and give them reviews online. Reviews are tough to get and highly valued. They are silent applause. Cultivate a reputation as a reviewer. I buy books from Amazon and review them there.

**A SENSE OF ACHIEVEMENT:** As you inch your way toward becoming a professional writer and find your niche in the world of writing, a sense of achievement will feed your spirit and give you joy. That buoyant outlook is another gift you can give to others. Following are ways I've tasted that sense of achievement:

**Role Modeling:** Once you become a person of influence, you can show other writers how dreams of fame and fortune can be embellished with other, non-conventional ways of sharing their writing talent.

On a more personal level, as you grow, you become a role model for family and friends. This is no little thing, especially as you age. One of the blessings writing offers is that it is an activity compatible with aging. As long as you can see, your mind is good, and your fingers work, you can write. When I'm in assisted living, my plan is to write the life stories of my compadres there. I will still be purposeful.

Demonstrating a zest for life through writing, no matter the challenges, sends positive messages to the young. Because of your joy and purpose, the fear of aging your loved ones harbor is tempered, and they view their own futures more positively. This is huge. I've observed it first hand.

My children brag about my writing accomplishments, mostly I suppose, because they are surprised. I suspect they view their futures more positively because of my enthusiasm and productivity. My four-year-old granddaughter carries Grandma GoGo's books around, looks at the pictures, and pretends to read. Perhaps she will write her own book someday because her grandma did. I collaborated with my eight-year-old grandson to write a book about dinosaurs, *Spiky and Dicky*. Soon after we had designed the cover, I observed him showing off his graphic design skills to his little sister. She was impressed. So was I.

**Judging Writing Contests:** This is a rewarding activity—an opportunity to nurture other writers. I built enough credentials over several years to qualify to judge. I keep a log of conferences and workshops attended, courses taken, publications, contest wins, and participation in writers' organizations and events so I can show I'm qualified.

**Giving:** My joy is enhanced by the possibility that you, my reader, will find a reason to write because of something I said. If you create a composition so wonderful that when someone reads it they marvel at your gift, my purpose is fulfilled. And if you learn and share what you learn, you will find joy. That prospect enriches my life.

**WRITERS AS THIEVES:** Writers steal through observation. Following is an account of an experience I had while at a writers' conference. I've shared this story in speeches and writings and in a couple of books because it illustrates how something ordinary can be made magical through the craft of writing:

At a writers' workshop in New York City, I took a break from an all-night writing marathon to sit in a diner at two a.m. drinking coffee. The Friday night crowd trailed in after a frenzied night of fun. Some patrons were decked out in nightclub garb. In contrast, I looked like a French cafe slouch in clothes comfortable enough to be classified as pajamas and hair resembling a cat toy.

Writers are thieves, and this was an opportunity to do serious stealing through observation. As young women paraded by in trendy clothes and wobbled in four-inch heels, testosterone-fueled young men in the next booth delivered their pickup line: "Oh my god! You are so beautiful. Oh my god!" They didn't say this to me, of course. I was still trying to lose baby fat from my firstborn child forty-eight years ago.

One young woman's mini dress had hiked up so high that the crotch of her thong was visible in the front and her bare ass in the back. The guys were so taken by thong girl that they pounded the table. Unable to contain themselves, they rose from their seats as if their butts were filled with helium. Omitting the "You are so beautiful," they said, "Oh, my god! Oh, my god! Oh, my god!" as they followed her down the aisle with struts that would have made John Travolta proud. About that time, I overheard a confounding conversation in the next booth.

A dazed young woman with matted hair that resembled a tangled mesh of fishing lures, wore Christmas lights as a necklace. Sitting with her head dangling perilously close to her catsup-covered french fries, she lamented to her male companions that her boyfriend would be furious with her for getting so-o-o wasted. One of these noble fellows comforted her by suggesting, "It'll be all right. He'll get over it." To prove his point he said, "I threw up on my girlfriend once, and she's still my girlfriend."

Such a statement is a writer's treasure—the up-side of writing. Let's explore the downsides and how to avoid them or at least to make the best of them.

*Chapter 3*

# Eliminating Distractions

*No part of writing is free of frustrations. The willingness to endure them sets you apart from other writers. The good news is you may have more opportunities to avoid them than you realize.*

Once a writer has defined success on his own terms, he is the architect of his role in the profession. If activities are too objectionable or frustrating, the definition can be redefined and goals adjusted accordingly. He may refuse to perform unpleasant tasks, temper their impact, or hire someone else to do them.

The following ideas show how to do that. Most are based on my personal experiences, and, in some cases, they are unconventional. I'm old, which is an excuse to do whatever the hell I want. My approach may or may not work for you. Do your own thing. I'm just sharing here.

**NARROWING THE SCOPE:** Publishing, marketing, and selling processes distract me from the joy of writing.

Such activities are all-consuming and do not give me pleasure. Nor do they deliver results. Also, many of them I'm not good at. So now, to be happy, I only dabble in them.

**Publishing:** I attended a workshop in New York City where I spent a week with experts polishing a pitch. Shortly thereafter, I had a pitch session with an agent at my first writers' conference. It did not go well. I didn't get to give the pitch. I had a pad of notes from a conference session I had just left. The agent must have assumed it contained notes for my pitch because he reached across the table, turned it over, slapped it down, and said, "No notes." He lectured me about the value of critique groups and then gruffly dismissed me five minutes into what was supposed to be a ten-minute session. I was embarrassed to walk out of the room while other writers were still in the middle of their pitches. The disappointment was worse than the dismissiveness. *So this is what it's like.* I cried on the elevator to my room, left the conference, and spent the rest of the day shopping. I would have gone home except I couldn't get a refund on the hotel room.

I went to the banquet that night only because I'd paid for the meal. I was about to leave early when someone started giving out awards for the writing contest, and I won one right off. After two more prizes and the top *crème de la crème* award, I sat there stunned. The agent sat at a table where I could look him in the eye as I took each award back to my table. He never looked up. A hard working dude, he was on his phone.

Soon after that incident, I redefined success and stopped pursuing agents or publishers, so I've only pitched once since then. The lady was nice and asked for my manuscript. After some consideration, I decided not to send it to her. Having discovered self-publishing, I had other plans. The process of finding an agent or publisher is a severe challenge. I admire those with the gumption and courage to endure it. I enjoy agents' speeches at conferences but am relieved I don't have to pursue them. I recommend pitching for others, though. Writers do find agents through this process, and it forces a writer to define the premise, theme, and general concept of his book.

**Marketing:** With few exceptions, I don't do marketing. It's an intense undertaking fraught with considerable unpleasantries as determined by a mellow, introverted, solitary soul like myself. When I get lonely, I turn on the porch light. Moths are my friends. So promotion is an abrasive social process that goes against my nature.

Since marketing and publishing activities mandated by the publishing world don't line up well with my innate abilities, I'm not going to do them, especially since I can't make enough money to make that unpleasant effort worthwhile. A brazen marketeer I'm not. I allow a month or two for marketing after a book is launched. From then on out, I only dabble in it. I'm off to writing the next book.

For writers who have a burning desire to sell books, who enjoy the process, and are willing to make the sacrifices selling requires, go for it—all of it. You are awesome. For those of you like me who would rather spend time organizing all your Band-Aids into one box, it's okay to narrow the scope of marketing efforts.

**Selling**: Most of my sales occur after speaking engagements. I put books on a table in the back of the room or on a coffee table with a box with a slit in it into which people can drop money. I tell the audience upfront that they are welcome to take a book. If they want to throw money at me, they can drop something into the box.

(On one occasion, someone put a hundred dollar bill in it.) I absorb the sales tax cost. I enjoy getting books into people's hands whether they pay for them or not.

**Book Signings:** These were fun at first. They made me feel "authory," which was nice. But if authors expect to sell a substantial number of books at one, they need a reality check unless they are famous or had something incredibly interesting happen to them, like . . .like. . .well, I can't think of anything fascinating enough.

A bookstore informed me at my first signing that the average number of books sold at their events was nine, even though signings were announced in the local paper. I beat the average with twelve, probably because I rarely sat down and badgered every person within hawking distance, which was against my nature. It was an incredibly uncomfortable situation. Since then, I've narrowed book signings to events that involve camaraderie with writer friends. The last time I did so, I sold eleven books in eight hours. I spent more money on a poster and decorating the table than I made selling books. The person on the right of me sold one book and the person on the left two. Reality.

**A Platform:** Serious writers set on appealing to agents and publishers are expected to have a social media platform that demonstrates they have a large group of followers eager and willing to buy their books. In spite of the hype about selling through social media, doing so is almost an impossible task and few writers are successful at it. You must not only manage the technology required and do constant, compelling updates, you must somehow collect and hold on to people. This is harder than it sounds. It takes a huge following (in the thousands) to impress a publisher.

With so much noise on the Internet, it is a challenge to stand out no matter what you do. Trying to do so can suck the life out of you. At a minimum, sites include: a website, a blog, Instagram, Twitter, Facebook, Pinterest, Google+, LinkedIn, Goodreads, Amazon, and an email group. Once the sites are set up, they must be maintained, which can be costly and a huge distraction from writing. And writers are encouraged to build relationships with others on their platforms. I can't imagine how much time all this would take. Just thinking about it makes me want a Snickers.

I briefly pursued a platform back when I accepted the industry goal of selling books and making money. I spent hours setting up and maintaining Facebook and LinkedIn accounts. As far as I know, I only sold two books. After seeing a presentation on how to use Pinterest, I spent two days trying to set up a site and failed. Pinterest made me cry. I dabbled in blogging, but the commitment to post every week was too much, and it never got off the ground.

My writer friends engaged in social media activities tell me they don't realize meaningful sales through their platforms. Some ask me to follow them. As enthusiastic as I am about supporting other writers, I don't do it. Doing so would be another distraction from writing.

In the end, I narrowed my scope to having a website, which is manageable for a technological idiot like myself. I carved out a month of my life to learn basic graphic design from Apple trainers. Then I paid GoDaddy $400 for enough training to make the site happen. By doing it myself, I can make changes without having to hire someone to do that for me. Check out my site at www.nikkihanna.com. Its existence is a minor miracle.

I'll take a lot of crap for making this statement, but I'm going to say it anyway. Unless you can afford to hire someone to do the platform work for you, or you enjoy the experience, you should reassess the hype about a platform and consider investing your time in activities you enjoy or at least those that deliver solid results.

**SUBMISSIONS:** Most submissions to magazines and other publications are denied. The writer gets a reject form letter, if he gets anything at all. For a while, Mondays were my designated submission days. That lasted only a couple of months. I dreaded Mondays and found myself performing all kinds of unpleasant tasks to avoid them. My house had never been cleaner. I was a dirt-diva rock star. The place is not so clean now because I rarely—extremely rarely—do submissions, except for an online publication of short stories, *eMerge*, that has published everything I've submitted.

Some writers plaster walls or fill files with reject letters. I throw them away in the garage. I don't want them in my house. I don't keep files on submissions, nor do I track the results from them.

This is just me. If you have a burning desire to be published, do submissions and never give up. My wish for you is that you prevail. And surely you will, to some degree, if you never give up. Just be smart about it and weigh the alternatives when allocating your time.

**TECHNOLOGY COPING STRATEGY:** I'm a cyber slacker. I have big fights with technology, and I usually lose, often after considerable abuse. I've learned to surrender when I cry. If you are a technological idiot like me and the only office machine you can work efficiently is a pencil sharpener, you will be challenged as a writer because technology isn't something you can ignore. Writing is dependent on it.

Since a certain level of technical involvement is required, amassing resources to support what must be done is vital. Apple, my MacBook support resource, has been my salvation. This company dedicates considerable resources to supporting writers through educational programs and help desk availability. I would not be where I am today as a writer without Apple.

Unless you enjoy technology-based activities, you might reassess the return on investment you get from doing them. Maybe you limit yourself to the absolute necessities and hire a geek for the rest so you can focus on creative activities, and so you don't cry.

**RUNNING A BUSINESS:** Any writer who sells books is running a business and all that implies. This is something you have to do. I would rather spend my time contemplating the role tape worms play in the scheme of nature. However, there's no getting around business when you're running a business.

**Keeping It Simple:** I use the sole proprietorship model. A limited liability company (LLC) is another alternative. I have a separate bank account and credit card to record revenue and expenses, and take only enough income tax deductions to cover revenue. (Taking a loss for too many years and deducting home office expenses often trigger IRS audits.) Writers should consult tax experts to determine their approach to business and tax issues.

**Sales Taxes:** This is a nuisance in my state. The website filing process is frustrating beyond belief, and customer service is non-existent. Filing the monthly sales tax report is the most frustrating part of my business.

I keep the sales tax process simple at the point of sale. I charge buyers a flat $10 for every book and pay the tax myself. The rest of my sales, even those through my website, are channeled through Amazon, and I use their sales reports to file taxes. They are essentially doing my bookkeeping for me.

**BALANCING ACT:** A person can do too much or too little of anything. A writer who puts all his energy into writing misses out on the benefits of sales. One who invests too much time in sales misses the opportunity to create his next masterpiece. Striking a balance between what a writer enjoys and what must be done to achieve his goals requires a deliberate strategy.

Facing the downsides of the writing profession head-on is necessary to find joy. This means writers must identify unpleasant activities they can stop doing—or at least minimize their impact—and reallocate that time to more pleasant tasks. I hope sharing my personal challenges does not discourage writers. My goal is to broaden their perspectives by showing how I moved beyond the activities that sucked the life out of me. When I do have to do one of these tasks, I make certain to reward myself with chocolate—since a puppy is not an option.

My wish for writers is that, through my sharing, they are encouraged to identify functions that are not pleasant, reevaluate their value, and explore how to soften their impact. By exposing my experiences, I risk the wrath of many in the profession who have talents I lack and who see things differently. That's okay. I'm up for that. I have confidence in my writing philosophy and strategy, and I believe they will work for others. The next chapter reveals why I am so bold.

*Chapter 4*

# Authorship—The Path to Achievement

*Remember this in moments of despair. If you find writing is hard, it's because it is hard.*—William Zinsser

If you are a new writer, consider your first few years as an apprenticeship. Learn everything you can about your profession. Aspire to achieve the level of *authorship*. Isn't that a lovely word, *authorship*? What does it mean?

It means you display the marks of an expert. It means inadequacies will not distract from what you create. It means you embrace the craft of writing—including the nuisances that make a big difference. It means you are bold and dare to confront barriers that obstruct the timid. It means you are courageous about expressing yourself and generous with your talent. It means you produce quality work that demonstrates you are serious about being a writer —that you are a professional.

How do you achieve the status of expert? How do you reach the level of *authorship*? The most constructive path is through learning. Before we talk about learning, let's consider what it means to an author.

**ACHIEVEMENT, A PATH TO EMOTIONAL RESILIENCE:** Accomplishments bring joy and contribute to a sense of purpose. The level of achievement to which one aspires is a personal decision. If your goal is to reach the expert level of *authorship*, you will be focused on achievement. Keep a record of every award, learning experience, and professional accomplishment. Some of these are appropriate for developing the "About the Author" section of your books; for bios requested by contests, publishers, and editors; and for folks introducing you. Observe this list blossom over time. When confidence waivers, look at it and marvel at how far you've come.

As you progress through years of continuous learning, this list will reflect your path to becoming an expert. At some point you will know you've achieved the level of *authorship*. When the writing world sends you into a funk—and it will—that list is a source of emotional resilience. Pull it out, study it, and know you are a writer. It says to you: "You know some stuff. You are accomplished. You are, by god, somebody."

**PATHWAYS TO LEARNING:** I would not be writing this book or standing before writers today sharing my writing experiences if I had not engaged in continuous learning. Since I started writing ten years ago, I've taken nine college courses, attended twenty-some writers' conferences and workshops, and read over fifty books on writing and publishing. I've read countless books of other genres and perused numerous writers' blogs. I don't say this to brag, but to make a point. After all those years of study, I'm still learning.

If a writer doesn't look back at his first book with embarrassment, he is not improving. So much learning has taken place that my first book, as lovely as it is, embarrasses me. For years, I was tempted to rewrite it. I didn't because I considered it the baseline of my work—evidence of progress. (I use examples from it to show writers I'm coaching how flawed my writing was when I started, before all that learning happened. This is so they don't feel so bad when they see all the redlines I put on their first chapter.) I did finally give the book new life last year by re-writing it, and now I share it with pride.

**The Genre Bounce:** Much can be learned by reading other writers in your genre. But reading and even studying other genres is also fruitful. I call this *the genre bounce.*

> As a nonfiction writer, my work improved immensely when I studied fiction. I borrowed the fiction narrative arc concept, applied it to a memoir, and the book blossomed. I used fictional character development techniques on real-life characters, and they came to life. I used dialogue in memoir to show—not tell. After learning how to describe fictional settings, I painted real ones with stunning results.
>
> While studying poetry, I learned to make the last word in a line a strong, deliciously descriptive one. After applying that to prose, my sentence structure improved. When I discovered the rhythm of poetry, I learned to incorporate rhythm into titles, phrases, and sentences and to enhance the flow of narrative.

Every book read will make you a better writer. When humbled by the impressive talent of experts, remember: *Your writing is your gift to give. Don't let someone else's rainbow overshadow your own.*

Many writers cherish every book they read and are horrified at the thought of mutilating one by bending corners, highlighting, underlining, and writing in the margins. I do all of these. It's part of devouring the material, taking it in.

When I discover something in a book I think will make my writing better or that I can use some way in the future, I note it on the inside cover. Before I put the book away, I put this information into my online Idea List, a file of writing suggestions I keep for future reference. I also keep a list of observed writing techniques for possible use in speeches, writing workshops, or books. I also keep lists of thoughts, fascinating words, unique names, and quotes.

I'm always on a quest for techniques, ideas, and wonderful words—magical, fabulous, descriptive words to use in unique ways. A writer is not allowed to plagiarize, but, in general, words are not copyrighted (although some are trademarked).

For example: I saw the word *feral* used in an interesting way in a book and used it myself to refer to children on spring break in Florida ("the feral children") and to describe love gone wrong ("love turned feral").

**Reading the Experts:** William Zinsser was an American writer, editor, literary critic, and teacher who taught at Yale University. Journalism professors use his book *On Writing Well* in their classes. He said, "Writing is learned by imitation. If anyone asked me how I learned to write, I'd say I learned by reading the men and women who were doing the kind of writing I wanted to do and trying to figure out how they did it." Stephen King said, "If you don't have time to read, you don't have the time or the tools to write." So read. A list of recommended readings is in the Appendix.

**Writers' Blogs:** Following successful writers on their blogs is a lucrative source of information about writing and the publishing industry. Peruse the blogs of your favorite authors and sign up as a follower for those that resonate with you. You will learn a lot and stay up to date on your profession. A writer's blog I followed is what put me on the road to self-publishing.

**Webinars and Podcasts:** Online searches, writers' groups, writers' blogs, and writing magazines are sources of information on webinars and podcasts. They are an inexpensive, convenient medium for learning.

**MARKS OF AN EXPERT:** The prerequisites to becoming an expert include those attributes that set a writer apart. An expert must have voice and style in spades.

**Voice:** In a panel discussion at a conference, publishers and editors were asked: "What is the most important quality you look for in a writer?" All seven panelists responded, "Voice." As a writer, your commodity is your voice.

What is voice? It is the literary fingerprint of the writer. Voice provides the zing. Voice serves up a symphony of words, quirky interpretations, and robust revelations of the writer's impressions. Voice is personal and individual. Voice means the writer writes like nobody else. Voice is what gives a composition personality and makes it memorable. Voice is elusive and too deep to cover here. Research it online, read about it, study it. Every book on writing talks about voice.

Some say voice is innate—you either have it or you don't. Not true. You can consciously cultivate voice. You must do so in a way that does not interject yourself into a fiction piece and take the reader out of the story.

Here are tools I use to introduce voice: the R*un-Though Process* (see Appendix) and my *Idea List* of words, phrases, quotes, sayings, and thoughts I've collected over time. Being careful not to plagiarize, I review the list, mold ideas into my own interpretations, and incorporate them into whatever I'm writing.

In the first three or four drafts, I'm *free flowing*—taking communion with myself. After about the fourth one, when the piece has evolved to the point of good organization and little clutter, I do an intense run-through that focuses entirely on finding my voice. This usually takes about two months.

Your voice will come from revising. Keep in mind, revising *is* writing, and a voice run-through *is* writing. Finding voice requires interjecting something that takes the writing to a higher level. This process is reflected in the Dedication of my playful, saucy book *Near Sex Experiences*. This Dedication sets the stage for the book:

**First Draft:** "Dedicated to Sam Elliott, a wonderful, sexy older man whom I have adored for years."

**With Voice:** "Dedicated to Sam Elliott, a fabulous seventy-one-year-old masculine piece of bravado and sensitivity who enters a scene with a rakish swagger, causing the air around him to dissipate as he holds the universe together."

---

**First Draft:** Dedicated to the men I've loved.

**With Voice:** Dedicated to the men I've loved. Because of them, when I'm asked to check a box for sex on forms, I draw my own box for *not pertinent*.

---

**First Draft:** Dedicated to my therapist, who saved me at a critical time.

**With Voice:** Dedicated to my therapist. When I mucked around in a funk and bared my soul, she had the self-discipline to not say, "Well, that was weird."

---

This verbiage reflects the tone and genre (humorous prose) of the book. It introduces a unique style, one that surprises the reader. No one would describe this dedication as trite. After reading the first dedication to Sam, readers are likely to read the rest of them and to anticipate reading the book.

Voice is about the writer's personality, emotions, tone, and how he portrays action. It is about such things as being witty, sarcastic, inspirational, or inventive. It is about potent words.

**Style:** The difference between voice and style is subtle. *Style* is broader and involves how a person writes. A composition is ornate, complex, long, and packed with imagery. Or it is sparse, simple, and conversational. A *style* might be described as academic, formal, and authoritative like David Grann or Jane Mayer while another is casual and light-hearted like Dave Barry and David Sedaris. One writer's style shows a preference for short choppy sentences and short paragraphs while another is lush with narration and rich with dashes and long, complex sentences. The long paragraphs and sentences adopted by Virginia Wolf are reflective of her style. Hemingway's short bursts and Stephen King's expressive prose are recognizable from just a few paragraphs. Nurture your natural style as it evolves while developing voice.

**Integrity:** Through the profession of writing, a person leaves a mark. Project the mark of an expert. Actions you take to achieve *authorship* feed your image. Learn the requirements of the profession. One of those is to be a person of integrity. Once you discover the perfect match of innate talents to the task at hand, apply them in a way that demonstrates good character. There is intense competition in the writing world. It's a matter of integrity to respect and honor the accomplishments of others as well as to relish your own.

**The Quality of Writing:** Readers recognize expert writing instantly. They also know bad writing when they see it. Sometimes its difficult for them to figure out what's wrong, but they know something is off. At other times, flaws are more obvious as in these examples:

> Ed panicked and turned when he heard a low, menacing voice coming from his rear.

> Suddenly the door opened slowly.

> The most common side-effect of a sleep drug is sleep.

> He's watching unsupervised TV.

> I dreamed I had insomnia.

> When Ike Turner died, a newspaper headline said, "Ike Turner beats Tina to Death."

> A kid trying to imitate something he saw on television said, "You want a piece of *meat*? Then I'm going to kick your *ask*."

I apologize for those. My sense of humor got away from me, but you get the point.

The next chapter talks about craft. For writers who want to be published, an acute awareness of craft is vital. If they self-publish, they alone are responsible for the quality of what is produced. Let's explore concrete solutions for writers determined to achieve the mark of an expert. If you are not up for that, agents, publishers, and others involved in the profession of writing will surely kick your *ask*.

# SECTION II

The Craft of Writing

*If polishing a manuscript makes you feel as though someone is doing a Riverdance in your head, you are not alone. But it is the writer's job to supply the shine that only revision, editing, and proofreading can deliver. Don't assume these functions are what someone else does. A shrewd writer knows review processes are intrinsic functions of writing, and he performs them himself before sending a manuscript to anyone else for their refinement.*

# Chapter 5

# Craft—The Concept

*Being a wordsmith is not just about hammering out pretty words—writers should be concerned more with using their words in an economical fashion to craft something beautiful. Beauty is not in the words, but in the images.*—Gordon A. Kessler

Significant craft is involved in writing, more than most new writers realize. You can just start writing, and you should because writing is one way to learn how to write. But you won't be writing well unless you study the craft. If your goal is to project an aura of professionalism, you must demonstrate craft. This shows a commitment to the art, builds writing muscles, and makes a writer's brilliance pop. Craft is a measure of competency, the foundation of *authorship*. However, when it comes to craft, there is an exception:

> Creating a life story trumps craft. It is not important that a memoirist produce a perfect book. It is just important that he have one. A flawed memoir boasts an intrinsic,

enduring charm all its own, one that reveals the essence of the writer and the subject. Most memoirs are written by amateurs who do not aspire to sell books. They should not allow concerns about craft to inhibit their work. The most important thing about a memoir is that it exists.

Craft carries considerable weight with agents and publishers. No one in this industry today has time to polish up an amateur's work when there are so many talented, masterful writers competing for the few key slots available for publication or awards. When an agent, publisher, or contest judge reads a submission, they know within the first few pages—maybe within the first few sentences—if a writer measures up in the arena of craft. If he does not, they'll move on to more expert writers, and it won't matter how wonderful the story is.

**EXPERTS ON CRAFT:** An important step in mastering craft is reading the experts. Every book you read by them will make you better. Here is a taste of that wisdom:

William Zinsser, in his book, *On Writing Well*, suggests this: "The secret to good writing is to strip every sentence to its cleanest components. Every word that serves no function, every long word that could be a short word, every adverb that carries the same meaning that's already in the verb weakens the strength of a sentence."

Stephen King, in his book, *On Writing*, advises: "Grammar is not just a pain in the ass; it's the pole you grab onto to get your thoughts up on their feet and walking."

Anne Lamott in b*ird by bird* says: "Write a shitty first draft." This allows the creative juices to flow, but at some point, you've got to follow up by polishing that shitty draft into something beautiful.

William Bernhardt says, "End every chapter on a critical moment. Put the resolution in the next chapter so readers will read on."

Angela Ackerman and Becca Puglisi in their book, *The Emotional Thesaurus,* speak about the *show—don't tell* principle: ". . .above all else, readers pick up a book to have an emotional experience. . .[Readers] don't want to be told how a character feels; they want to experience the emotion for themselves."

Marcia Riefer Johnston, author of *Word Up* asked: "What critic will be impressed by your mastery of craft? The critic with the power to hold you back." That could be an agent, a publisher, a contest judge, or a reviewer.

The nature of craft is tedious, which is why so many people avoid it. Embracing it is the key to standing out from the masses. Let's talk about craft.

**LAYERS OF CRAFT:** I apologize for going all textbook on you, but you need to know this. There are three layers of craft:

**(1) The Rules:** These include proper grammar, punctuation, spelling, word use, sentence structure, writing technique, and such mechanics as formatting and presentation. Rules are outlined in style books, such as *The Chicago Book of Style* and Strunk and White's *The Elements of Style* and in the *Modern Language Association's Standard Format.* There is some controversy over certain rules but, in general, they are well-established.

**(2) Preferences of Experts:** These requirements aren't necessarily right or wrong, but experts care about them. They include such things as avoiding adverbs, using one space at the end of a sentence instead of two, and applying the Oxford comma. It's a good idea to go with what is trending with publishers.

**(3) The Finesse of Writing:** This includes writing techniques and nuances that set a writer apart. In fiction, craft requires vivid, emotive writing rich with passion, emotion, intensity, power, and a clever plot. This means skillful presentation of voice, showing rather than telling, point of view technique, effective structure, brilliant descriptions, and other writing techniques that draw readers into the story. In most nonfiction and how-to books, craft involves the ability to persuade the reader to act or to convince him of something. In memoir, it is the ability to bring a person to life on the printed page.

**Breaking Rules:** Craft requirements and common practices don't always mean alternatives are wrong. Rules are controversial among experts, and there are reasons to break them. Writers often violate rules in the interest of style and practicality. (An incomplete sentence may be intentional.) In general, though, complying with the rules of craft is important to agents, publishers, and writing professionals as well as to readers.

You may ask, "With all these rules and requirements, Nikki Hanna, how can you propose the premise of *write whatever the hell you want and write it whatever way you want?"* The answer is simple. You absolutely can disregard the rules if you choose. Writers do it all the time. It's a personal choice, and a brave one. Just don't expect to be recognized as a professional writer if you are doing it out of ignorance or a disregard for craft.

**UP-FRONT CRAFT DECISIONS:** Following are decisions a writer must make before serious writing begins. For a memoirist, these decisions are best addressed after the first draft. You'll understand this after reading the next chapter.

**Premise/Theme:** These terms are sometimes used interchangeably. They are kindred spirits to an elevator speech or a soundbite. Generally, the *premise* comes first. It is the central idea of the story, the kernel that describes the overall concept. It delivers a powerful punch in a single sentence or, at most, two or three. The premise of this book is that writers should write whatever the hell they want and in whatever way they want. In fiction, the premise usually identifies the protagonist and a threatening antagonist, gives a sense of setting, reveals conflict, tells what's at stake, and hints at how the action will play out. That's a lot of work for a few sentences, but it is doable.

The *theme* of a story evolves from that premise. It refers to the underlying message of the story. Many writers have a sense of the theme when they begin to write, but themes can present organically as writing progresses. Sometimes they mutate as the story unfolds. There may be more than one theme. In this book finding joy and purpose and achieving *authorship* are themes.

If someone asks you what you are writing and you can't immediately tell them, you've not written down the premise and theme. Articulating them up front guides the writing and provides verbiage to explain to agents, publishers, and other curious inquirers what you are writing about.

**Inciting Incident:** This is the navel of a book, an event so intense and compelling it is the first thing that comes to a reader's mind when he thinks back on the story. It's the shower scene in *Psycho*, Robert Redford getting shot in *The Natural*, Shirley MacLaine's raging rant at nurses in *Terms of Endearment,* Harrison Ford in *Indiana Jones* running from a rolling boulder, and Normandy Beach in *Private Ryan*. An inciting incident is so vital to the story that it is generally introduced up front to provide the action and intensity that makes a reader want to read on. Make certain your book has a well-placed and compelling inciting incident.

**Structure:** Whether fiction or nonfiction, a book needs a framework to support the strategic sequencing of events. Structure is the skeleton of a story—the architecture. Even poets use structure to shape verse.

Numerous approaches exist for creating story structure. Fiction writers are taught to create a narrative arc. Apprentice writers, regardless of genre, would do well to study this concept. Most writers define structure up front through outlining, storyboarding, or some other method. Others let the structure evolve as the story unfolds. Either way, consciously determining structure at some point is important. (Read Bill Bernhardt's *Story Structure* and Jack Bickham's *Scene & Structure*.) Structure is facilitated through transitions. More about that later.

Memoir is adaptable to the narrative arc structure of fiction. Other nonfiction, including how-to and information sharing books, don't have the complicated story components of fiction. The Table of Contents is helpful for organizing them.

Many variations of structure are available to the writer. Explore them in the books you read. Here are examples:

> In my memoir *Red Heels and Smokin'—How I Got My Moxie Back*, I used this structure: (1) start with a defining moment, (2) go back and show the build-up to it, (3) show the aftermath and ultimate consequences and resolution. (This works well in memoir when the person experienced a traumatic incident or a defining moment that changed everything. Putting that incident up front pulls the reader in. It sets up the historical backdrop that follows, which then sets the stage for subsequent chapters that lead to the resolution.)

---

> A popular model, almost always apparent in a TV series, goes like this: Everything is good. A problem surfaces.

The situation gets worse as characters try to resolve it. Just as the solution looks hopeful, a major crisis materializes right before the last commercial. Finally, there is resolution. All is rosy. Even reality shows and HGTV remodels reflect a semblance of this model.

**Beginning, Middle, and End:** Whatever structure the writer chooses, every story/chapter/scene should have these three parts. Even nonfiction, including memoir, is adaptable to three sections. This does not mean a writer should follow the "speaker philosophy," which is to tell the audience what you're going to tell them, tell them, and then tell them what you told them. Don't do that. Do this:

**Beginning:** The honeymoon period with a reader lasts about two pages so these pages have a lot of work to do. The first sentence must be brilliant and masterfully draw in the reader. (Examples in Appendix) The first few pages might include an inciting incident, be filled with action, give a sense of time and place (setting), introduce characters, reveal what they want and obstacles to obtaining it. The central theme is articulated, or at least hinted at. The beginning introduces tension, curiosity, conflict, and intrigue. It wows the reader.

**Middle:** The middle must not suck. Plots and sub-blots—rich with events, suspense, and conflict—are active. Characters evolve. The story thickens. The writer keeps the momentum going by continuously upping the stakes for the characters and introducing twists and turns that surprise readers. This is the longest part of the book.

**End:** The story culminates with a crisis and then a dynamic climax, which involves hit after hit of action. Post-climax, when that crisis is resolved, is cleanup time. Show how characters are changed by what happened. Give the reader closure, some emotional resonance or takeaway. Writers call this the denouement.

Keep it succinct. It can be feel-good stuff or a tragedy. A loose end can hint at another book in a series.

**Tense:** Early on, the writer determines the tense in which to write. Once determined, he is generally consistent with tense. Exceptions are okay if done strategically and executed so they don't jar the reader. Tense is more complicated than most writers realize. Do an online search, and you'll learn how to determine the best tense for your project and how to manage it. Notice use of tense in the books you read.

**Person:** Another strategic up-front decision is whether to write in first, second, or third person First person is most appropriate for memoirs; second person for how-to, self-help, and informational nonfiction; and third person for fiction.

**First Person:** I, we, me, my, mine, us, our, ours
**Second Person:** you, your, yours
**Third Person:** he, she it, they, them, him, his,
her, hers, their, theirs

Consistency of person is important, but there are reasons to make exceptions. Variations exist and, like tense, this is more complicated than you might think. Study up.

**Point of View (POV):** A story must be written from someone's point of view. The POV is primarily the main character or a narrator, but it can change. Identify the POV in the first few sentences of each chapter or scene, and have only one. No "head-hopping" unless done for strategic reasons. Use the person's name the first time they are mentioned and then use a personal pronoun for the rest of the chapter/scene. POV tactics are crucial to good writing. Do a search online and, again, study up.

**Settings:** Readers need a sense of place, time, and environment. Settings orient readers. Every scene requires some indication of where and when it is happening. Sometimes this involves a subtle clue and other times a glorious description. Settings are hard-working writer tools. They paint pictures, put up backdrops, set stages, hint at backstories, and string visual clues together. They establish geography, culture, climate, weather, social context, history, and the time and season of events.

Go through your entire book looking for opportunities to add depth and context to the story through setting descriptions. Use metaphor, simile, and visually stimulating words. Consider this simile that describes a front porch: *Flowers were positioned on each side of the steps as though they were earrings.*

This is brilliant. Not only is the description clever, it says something about who lives there, a woman most likely. What if the author had said the flowers in the pots were dead? That changes the visual drastically as well as what it implies about the occupant. What if this author had stopped at steps? The zing of "as earrings" is lost. To this day, when I see flower pots on each side of front-porch steps, I think of them as earrings. Those two words do a lot of work.

Setting supports the architecture of the story, introduces sensory interpretations, orients readers, and draws them in. (Read Mary Buckham's book, *Writing Active Setting.*)

**CHARACTER DEVELOPMENT:** A serious writer will invest considerable up-front time developing characters. He will create a profile for every major one and determine the purpose of minor ones. This profile will include information on the characters' past, present, and her hopes and dreams for the future as well as internal and external qualities. After profiles are developed, a writer knows his characters intimately. This information guides their behavior as the story unfolds.

Strategically time the introduction of characters and use them to advance stories. Don't limit yourself to descriptions of characters. Bring them to life through actions, traumatic events, and challenging recoveries. Introduce profound consequences for their decisions. William Bernhardt said, "Few books will succeed if the protagonist is not dealing with something psychologically or emotionally in addition to confronting the external problem." Here are tactics for character development, some of which I learned in his fiction workshops. These gave me a genre bounce that improved my memoir and nonfiction writing:

> Leave no doubt about who is the main character. Keep a laser-like focus on him. Give him special abilities and uncommon traits. Have him harbor a secret.
>
> Characters are most appealing when they are complicated. A deeply flawed character with a big heart is captivating. Create heroes who are not perfect and villains who have redeeming qualities.
>
> Portray primary characters as sympathetic and vulnerable—even the bad guys—so readers relate to them. Nothing is more appealing than an underdog.
>
> Burden every primary character with a discontent.
>
> Interject internal and external conflict. Characters are most interesting when they irritate each other.
>
> Introduce collusion. Conspiracy is intriguing.
>
> Give characters mannerisms, quirks, and ways of speaking that reveal their personalities.
>
> Convey motives behind the actions of primary characters. Even fictional characters must have a past. What they experienced shaped them and influences future behavior.

Diverse characters add texture to a story. Make each one distinctive and one of them a troubling wreck of a person.

**Primary Characters:** Create three-dimensional players (each one with a past, present, and future). Avoid stereotypes.

Readers want a lead player who says things a boring person would not, who acts in a way an average person would not, and who bucks up when most would quake.

Primary characters require *character arcs*. This means they experience emotional growth and change over the course of the story. (Read Bill Bernhardt's book *Creating Character*.)

**Minor Characters:** Less important characters are in a story for practical reasons. They give the main ones someone to talk to. Dialogue reveals thoughts and informs readers. Soon after studying character roles in a workshop, I came across an old *Gunsmoke* show and saw Chester's role in a new light. It was clear his purpose was not limited to comic effect or sidekick support. He expressed observations, gave information, and provided the viewer with details through dialogue with Marshal Dillon and others. Chester played a key roll in advancing the story.

Supporting and minor players require only enough description to serve their purpose, add interest, move the story forward, and provide information through dialogue. They don't necessarily have to have a name, and they stay in the story only as long as needed. Make them interesting, though, like Chester. Don't create cardboard characters.

**Comical Characters:** A comical or zany sidekick provides a superb foil for a protagonist. Consider the comedic effects Chewbacca brought to *Star Wars*. A comical henchman to a villain provides opportunities to add spice or to soften the blows of dastardly antics. Even a serious book can benefit from a quirky, bungling character or a smart aleck who adds a dash of sarcastic humor like the Doc Holliday character in *Tombstone*. His comment to an adversary, "If I thought you weren't my friend, I don't think I could bear it," is classic. Reflect on the coupling of characters in sitcoms and movies. There is almost always that oddball person connected in some way to the main character.

**Character Descriptions:** Weave character descriptions throughout the story. Don't unload them all at once. Show attributes through behavior and dialogue as well as through narration. A reader knows a lot about a wife who says, "I hate NASCAR and Bruce Willis." They also know a lot about her husband. Demonstrate physical, mental, and spiritual depth. Instead of describing a person as sensitive, say: "Donna believes the purpose of bread is to feed ducks. She doesn't fish because of an uncontrollable urge to rescue bait." Or, better yet, reveal her sensitivity through action or dialogue.

Present primary characters from physical, mental, and behavioral perspectives.

- **Describe external qualities:** appearance, clothes, hair, eyes, skin color, expressions, gait, weight.

- **Describe internal qualities:** witty, ambitious, friendly, staid, adventurous, mean, quirky, criminal, anxious, fun.

- **Describe characters through their worlds:** home, vehicle, pets, workplace, associations, lawn, community, sofa, diet.

Describe physical characteristics in colorful ways rather than literally. Depict a person with big ears as having "ears like suicide car doors." Someone brilliantly portrayed the essence of Alec Baldwin by how he walked: *He has the unbending, straight-armed gait of someone trying to prevent clothes from rubbing against sunburned skin.*

More craft is disclosed in the next chapters. This detail may make your head hurt but, trust me, it'll hurt so good.

# Chapter 6

# Craft—Writing 101

*When in doubt, have two guys come through the door with guns.*—Raymond Chandler

After the last chapter, I know what you're thinking. *Nikki Hanna tells me to find joy in writing and then lays all this craft crap on me.* You can opt out of the craft crap and write on any level you desire. Enjoy. Have fun. But if you see something you wrote published in a magazine, or climb up on a stage to receive an award for winning a contest, or hold a splendid published book in your hands with your name as author splashed across the front of it, you will know that craft matters. It is what got you there.

Such accomplishments are not for everyone. Do your own thing. Find your joy wherever it lives, and know that craft does not matter in the first draft. It is free-flowing magic. Take Anne Lamott's advice that it's okay to write a shitty one. Rules don't apply to a first draft. So go ahead. Have some fun. Write a really shitty first draft Lamott style.

**THE DRAFT PROCESS:** Michael Crichton said, "Books aren't written—they're rewritten. . . .It is one of the hardest things to accept, especially after the seventh rewrite hasn't quite done it." For me it's more like thirty re-writes.

If you are like most writers, there will be many drafts. One writer described multiple drafts this way: "I beat that manuscript like it were a rented mule." It's not unusual for a writer to complete twenty to fifty drafts, each one adding another layer of polish. If you find this hard to believe, look at the *run-through* and *sweeps* processes illustrated in the Appendix as well as the editing suggestions in *Chapter 7*. Draft work, called *revision* by professionals, is typically spread over several years. Revision *is* writing, and drafts are the heart of writing.

The first draft is freeform. If you are writing memoir, take communion with yourself and write whatever you want. No one is going to see it. You are the audience. This is your opportunity to vent and brag. Even if you're writing fiction, you are the audience in the first draft stage as you create characters and shape the story. You may have an outline to guide you, but you can still write freely. In future drafts that evolve into manuscripts, the audience becomes your target. You'll need to know more about craft to capture them and hold them.

**BASIC WRITING PRINCIPLES:** Following are important methods every serious writer should master.

**Active vs Passive Voice:** In *Chapter 4*, I talked about the author having voice. Here voice comes up again, but this time it relates to sentences. To write strong, writers are advised to use active voice. However, passive voice is not technically wrong, and it comes in handy to make a sentence work or to vary sentence structure. Just don't overuse it. In general, it's best if the flavor of the writing is strong.

With active voice, the subject does the action. In passive voice, the object of the verb does the acting. If the prospect of finding passive situations through grammatical analysis makes your head hurt, lighten up. Identifying passive voice is easy. Do a search (find) on *be, by, being,* and *been.* These words almost always signal passive voice. *Was, were,* and *is* may also do so.

The verb determines if a sentence is active or passive. Eliminate as many passive sentences as you can. A simple way to do that is to put the subject at the beginning of the sentence. Note the presence of *was, were, is, be,* and *being* in the passive sentences below in contrast to the stronger verbs in the active sentences.

> **Passive:** The wedding dress *was ironed* by Mattie.
> **Active:** Mattie *ironed* the wedding dress.
>
> **Passive:** Mashed potatoes *were eaten* by Mary.
> **Active:** Mary *ate* mashed potatoes.
>
> **Passive:** The runway *will be graced* by beautiful models.
> **Active:** Beautiful models *will grace* the runways.
>
> **Passive:** That style *is being worn* by everyone.
> **Active:** Everyone *wears* that style.

Although *was, were,* and *is* might signal passive voice, not all sentences using them are passive. These verbs are necessary to establish tense. Don't try to take them all out. The enthusiasm in the writer community for eliminating passive voice is excessive. One so-called expert said *was* is death to a memoir. I'm still scratching my head over that one. Just try writing a memoir in past tense without using *was.* That would be weird.

**Show—Don't Tell:** When writers use *seem, feel, felt, knew, learned, looked, hoped, noticed, saw, heard, thought, realized, guessed, wondered,* and other words describing internal sentiments, they are telling instead of showing. Telling is necessary. Don't be afraid to use exposition (a big word for telling). It is not wrong, but too much telling is trite and boring. Showing draws the reader into the story so he can taste the emotion. Consider these examples:

> **Tell:** The alarm went off. I was so *tired*. It *seemed* as though I had just fallen to sleep. I *felt* like crying, but I *knew* I had to get back to work.

> **Show:** The alarm blasted me awake. My body quaked, eyes squinted. After only two hours of sleep, my heart pounded at the shock of the intrusion. As I recalled the events of the previous day, tears formed in the corners of my eyes. I fought them back. Forcing myself out of my nest, I stumbled to the bathroom like a squirrel looped on fermented berries. The ugly grimace on the face in the mirror shouted, "Go back to bed." But work owned me.

---

> **Tell:** He *looked* mad. I *was* afraid, but I *knew* I had to stand my ground.

> **Show:** His face transformed into a savage grimace. His piercing eyes glared, and his chin quivered. The hair stood up on the back of my neck as I squared myself for the attack.

In addition to narration as demonstrated here, a writer can accomplish serious *show—don't tell* through dialogue.

**Economical Writing:** This may be the most important advice a new writer will ever get. Cut out every unnecessary word and any sentence or paragraph not necessary to the story. Failure to do so will show up on the first page and scream "amateur." Be brutal. Writers call this "killing your darlings," those precious, eloquent creations that make you feel as though you are on the verge of a Shakespearean experience. And don't produce anything that is TLTR (Too Long to Read). Size matters. Here are some soft benchmarks:

- A sentence with more than one add-on phrase is too long.
- A paragraph over half a page is too long.
- A chapter over ten pages in nonfiction is too long. In memoir and fiction, even shorter chapters are best.
- A book over 300 pages is too long.

If you find yourself skipping sections when proofing because you cannot deal with reading them again, consider that a signal your reader will skip them as well.

At some point, a smart writer will go through his manuscript and eliminate every unnecessary word, sentence, paragraph, chapter, or possibly even a character. He will reconsider every adverb and adjective. Sentences are often stronger without them. Compare these two sentences. Which one is stronger and more reader friendly?

My mom was an extremely devoted mother with an exceptionally vibrant personality and a very responsible nature. She worked really hard and took very good care of us.

My mom was a devoted mother with a vibrant personality and responsible nature. She worked hard and took good care of us.

In most cases, when forced to make cuts to meet word-count limits in contests or articles, the work is better, richer, and tighter. Flowery, excessive writing is called *purple prose*. It will get a submission thrown into a reject pile quicker than anything. (See *Sweeps—Find and Fix* in the Appendix for words subject to deletion. Some of them will surprise you.)

**Sentence Structure:** The first sentence of a book, a chapter, and a paragraph must dazzle the reader and draw him in. The last sentence of a paragraph should say something important and provide a smooth transition to the next paragraph.

Poets are taught to make the last word in every line a strong, important, deliciously descriptive one for a reason. The punch. This principle works on sentences. William Zinsser said, "The punch word should come at the end of a sentence."

Do a run-through focused on going over every sentence and improving it. Review the order of sentences within paragraphs and sequence them properly. Take out redundant sentences. Every one must contribute, serve a purpose, advance the story, and have a reason to be.

Vary the length and style of sentences. Keep them short where possible. Avoid *run-on sentences* (compound sentences without a conjunction tying them together) and *compound sentences* (those with phrases added on making them *complex sentences)*.

If you stumble over words, take the hint. Your readers will as well. Rewrite the sentence or take it out.

**Narration vs Exposition:** *Narration* involves the voice of the point of view character moving the story forward. *Exposition* is the author setting forth information or describing something or someone. Both should be economically applied and spread out, nestled in between dialogue. Readers will skip paragraphs if an author data dumps through these.

**Dialogue:** Use conversations to reveal the character of a person, to show action, to express emotions, and to advance the story. Don't be afraid to use dialogue in memoir. It brings characters and stories to life. Some writers tell fiction stories almost entirely through dialogue. This is challenging to do and it is tiring for readers. Most readers prefer the interjection of some narration and exposition.

Every character should have a distinct identity that is recognizable by what they say and how they say it. The reader should be able to identify characters by how they talk.

For dialogue tags (called *attributes*), stick with "said" and "asked" most of the time. When only two people are talking, few tags are needed. There is considerable technique to writing dialogue. (Read William Bernhardt's *Dynamic Dialogue*)

**Pacing:**. Continuous emotion or action exhausts the reader and makes him feel as though he has been handcuffed to Kevin Hart. Follow high-energy action scenes with calmer ones. Like with music, mellow points make the dynamic ones more effective. Take your reader on a roller coaster ride.

**Rhythm and Flow:** Rhythm is what makes a book a page-turner. Reading the written word out loud reveals its cadence. Awkward sentences, poor word selection, and unwieldy syntax (word order) stop readers. Smoothing the flow from word to word, sentence to sentence, and paragraph to paragraph keeps them reading. However, when the same sentence structure is repeated over and over (unless done intentionally for effect), rhythm becomes boring.

**Sharing Wisdom:** A story that incorporates lessons learned will captivate readers. A memoir writer gives a gift to readers when he has the courage to expose his mistakes and reveal the lessons they evoked. Share such wisdom without being preachy. Fictional characters who change over time also have messages to share that add depth and meaning to a story and give the reader a takeaway.

**Humor:** No matter how serious the tone of a book, it can benefit from a dash of humor. Don't be afraid of it. William Zinsser, a serious, scholarly writer, advised: "If something strikes me as funny in the act of writing, I throw it in. . .I assume a few other people will find it funny. . . ."

**Thought Shots:** These are character or narrator thoughts, usually expressed in italics. They can be used to reveal the personality of the person having the thought and to convey vital, punchy, humorous information. To be effective, they must be relevant and fascinating, not trite. A writer who uses them should be careful not to take the reader out of the story.

**Spotlights:** Using a short, choppy sentence, typically in the midst of longer ones or at the end of a paragraph, is a technique that effectively surprises readers. Spotlights are especially effective at delivering bold or humorous statements. This often involves making an obvious observation in a clever way. Examples: "Mavis went psycho." "I'm not obsessive." "It freed his freak." "He was girl stuck." See a spotlight example on page 157: "Fashionistas don't write."

**Climax:** There should be a lot happening on several fronts during the climax. Readers feel cheated if conflicts are too simple, obvious, and easily resolved. A climax may involve several scenes—short, action-oriented, vibrant scenes. A climax should answer the question: Did the main character get what he wanted? (Read William Bernhardt's *Perfect Plot*.)

We are not done with craft yet. The next chapter presents writing strategies that cause a writer to standout. These tactics are crucial to moving out of the amateur mode and into expert status. They represent the essence of good writing. Apply them, and your writing will shine.

## Chapter 7

# Craft—The Edge

*Like it or not, writing is a competition. If you aspire to be published, buck up, get your game on, and dare to stand out.*

The supply of writers significantly exceeds the demand. To be competitive in any situation, a writer must stand out from the crowd.

**HOW TO STAND OUT:** Mastering the following components of craft give a writer an edge.

**Titles:** Maximizing the impact of titles is a skill that sets a composition apart. Unique, enticing titles are memorable. In nonfiction, including memoir, chapter titles and sub-titles are included in the Table of Contents. Make them a fireworks display of popping, seductive, clever, and descriptive titles. The Table of Contents sells books. In contests, clever titles help a judge remember the entry.

Fiction chapters normally don't have titles and are limited to a number and perhaps a notation of time and place.

**Name Selection:** A name defines a character instantly. Name choices have broad implications. A smart writer keeps a list of fascinating, memorable names. He uses ordinary names only for ordinary people. The difference between Nancy and Pepper is significant. Baxter is old; Jason is not. Austin is a country boy, and Hawk a detective.

Knuckles is a big dog, and Howie a hyped-up Yorkie. You can play around and call a fluffy white little thing Killer for fun, and it would probably work, but Rufus conjures up ugly, and there ain't no changing that. He snores, drools, farts, and his tongue hangs out of the side of his mouth. Then there is GiGi, a bouncy little yipper.

Names define the age of characters. Hank and Mable are on Social Security. Jason and Brittney just got engaged. Aiden and Bella are starting kindergarten. Avoid names that start with the same letter or have similar pronunciations. They confuse readers.

**Word Selection:** Most writers have heard this expression from Mark Twain: *The difference between the almost right word and the right word is the difference between the lightning bug and the lightning.*

One word may make a piece hum and another make it sing like an opera star. Isn't *ashen* more disturbing than *pale*? *Chilling* gives me goosebumps. *Scary* does not. There is a distinct difference between *persuade* and *convince* and between *famous* and *notorious*.

Navigating the world of words and orchestrating their use is how authors convey their intended meaning. Doing so is an art. Word choice sets a writer apart. Examples:

Instead of *home,* consider *hovel, cottage, mansion, bungalow, pad, crib*

Instead of *little,* consider *petite, lithe, willowy, dainty, elfin*

Instead of *big,* consider *Amazonian, massive, towering, enormous, colossal*

Paint a picture with words. Use colorful details and brilliant descriptions of characters, settings, and emotions. Use finesse and don't overdo.

- Describe wine as *articulate, complex, nutty,* or as *prancing grapes* (maybe that's a tad over the top)

- Describe memories as *keen, raw, cruel, delightful, fuzzy, poignant,* or *haunting*

- Describe a wine bar as a *luau of exotic concoctions* (borderline over the top)

- Describe something old as *a fossil*

Make a thesaurus your word fairy and the dictionary your guru. Do a run-through and pick just the right words. Francine Prose in her book, *Reading Like a Writer,* recommends: "Put every word on trial."

Don't try to impress with complicated narrative and big words. Never pick a big word because it is bigger, choose it because it is better. (Read Vivian Cook's *All in a Word: 100 Delightful Excursions into the Use and Abuse of Words* and Theodore A. Rees Cheney's *Getting the Words Right.*)

**Hooks:** Become a master of hooks—a tool with the potential to build strong connections with readers. Hooks are powerful because they are memorable. Example:

I've heard many sermons over the years and remember the message of only one. The minister used a hook. It had a rhythm to it. He said it over and over while preaching about meeting obligations when you don't feel like it. He said: "Do it anyway. Do it—and then some."

Years later, these two statements are still in my head. This hook defined my work ethic and drove a blossoming career. I used it to motivate employees when times were tough. I used it to instill a sense of responsibility in my children. I use it today to encourage grandchildren when it is important they do something they don't want to do.

Hooks convey themes and messages that stick with the reader. Many have rhythm. Hook the reader in the first few chapters and then hook him again later. If done well, a story hook will stick in a reader's head—perhaps forever.

**Mantras:** People often repeat crisp, snappy sayings that reflect their view of the world and that help them cope. Such expressions are derived from self-talk and are intensely meaningful to whoever says them. One teenage girl says, "I'm a really big thing," to defy insecurities, and another says, "I have issues," to excuse failures. If a character says, "The plan is that there is no plan," a reader expects that the person lives a free and spontaneous life, and they will anticipate reading more. A mantra can be a theme for an entire memoir or for a chapter.

A mantra that contributed to my surviving a career in corporate America and single parenthood proved to be a powerful coping mechanism: "This, too, shall pass." Another one helped me focus when I became overwhelmed: "Work the problem, Nik. Just work the problem." Weighty experiences inspired both of these mantras. When I say, "Sometimes I do things I shouldn't" and "I'm not a nice person," I'm justifying brave or irreverent behavior.

While driving a stock car, my son used a mantra to stay focused when things became precarious: "Drive, Marty. Just drive." I found myself repeating it in the stands as I watched him weave his way through masses of careening cars.

A mantra is a formidable writing tool for ferreting out a person's past and creating curiosity about his future. The source of mantras explains behavior. When interviewing people for memoir, seek out mantras and the stories behind them. Ask, "What do you say to yourself when something bad happens and you must be strong?" Introducing mantras into fiction adds depth to a character and creates curiosity:

> A character may say a few times throughout a book, "Don't affect me none." This suggests a coping strategy learned from a prior experience. The reader has to wonder what happened in the character's past that causes him to separate himself from what is going on in the moment. The writer has set the stage for a backstory and has foreshadowed how the character will respond to events in the future.

> Mantras can be a source of tension. For example: A character occasionally says, "It's raining men, hallelujah!" Her pal stopped believing it was raining men when she turned thirty and disco went out of style. These women are out of sync. Tension. Maybe conflict.

**Metaphor and Simile:** These are forms of figurative language that make comparisons between two different things. Be stingy with them so they remain special.

Shakespeare's, "The world is your oyster," is metaphor. Other examples are: "The road was a ribbon." "She is a vulnerable lamb." "An orange peel is fruit upholstery."

What distinguishes a simile is that it includes one of these words: *like, as if, as though, or similar to*. To create simile, put yourself in the situation of the character and consider instances when you witnessed a similar incident. To describe the eyes of a person in a precarious position, I recalled situations I had witnessed:

> . . . eyes like those of a drowning child

> . . . eyes like those of a woman being weaned from
> a respirator

I chose only one. A general rule in writing is to avoid doubling up when you have multiple examples of something. Pick the best one and use it. With two, they both lose their effectiveness.

**Elicit Emotion:** Passion is expressed through sentiment, which elicits an emotional response from the reader—a tear, a chuckle, anxiety, curiosity, joy, peace, pleasure. This is done by giving key characters the following:

- Something to care about, something to want
- Something to lose
- Something to dread, something at stake, something
  to suffer (Example: like snakes to Indiana Jones)
- Obstacles and threats
- Things to learn so characters change over time

Causing a reader to experience emotion is the primary objective of writing. Radicalizing a character's responses to emotional situations everyone relates to grabs readers.

When a vulnerable character overcomes fear, readers root for them and wish they could be that brave. Loss is a shared human condition. Portray unique responses to it. Betrayal is another situation rife with opportunities for delivering intense emotions and uncommon responses that fascinate readers and make them feel. Put a betrayal in your book and relish the intrigue and the punch it dishes up.

**Incorporate the Senses:** A wise writer will go through his story looking for opportunities to integrate the five senses into the text and to describe them brilliantly. Taste, sight, touch, smell, and hearing make a reader feel present. The aggravation of a cricket chirping in a closet, a dog barking in the distance as someone is being murdered, heat so intense a character wipes sweat off his forehead with his sleeve and looks good doing it, the softness of a robe or stiffness of a starched shirt as a man embraces a woman, the copper-penny taste of morning breath, and the smell of cat litter as one enters a house all add dimension to a story. Include some sort of sensory response in every scene.

**Emphasize Feelings:** No story will resonate with readers without conveying emotional depth.

A man in one of my memoir workshops wrote a factual account about riding his horse to school as a child. It was trite. He didn't even reveal the horse's name. I asked him the name and how he felt about his horse, and his eyes glazed over. Turns out, he had a strong emotional attachment to the horse. He added that perspective to his story and came back the next day with a gripping piece so moving it had the workshop participants in tears when the horse, Thunder, died at the end.

———————————

In the 1940s, when asked how many children they had, it was not unusual for women to answer in terms of "surviving children." My parents lost three children. The depths of Dad's feelings around those events were revealed when he watched my brother wrestle with his giggling toddler. Dad said, "You shouldn't get too attached to her. You could lose her."

This elicits an emotional response from me every time I read it, and I've read it fifty-some times while developing my memoir. And it still moves me today. It is that powerful. Those words reflect Dad's view of the world and explain his life-long emotional detachment.

For memoir, dig deep for such historical, biographical treasures. For fiction, create them. Show how and why a character behaves as he does. Feelings are where the magic resides. They are the driver of behavior, the heart of a story, the essence of a person, and a writer's goldmine.

**A Stand-Out Story:** How to write a compelling story everyone will want to read is beyond the scope of this book. Nevertheless, here is a list of subjects a writer would do well to master in order to deliver a fascinating, memorable book that stands out:

- An unusual storyline
- A defined premise, a theme, and strong messages
- A narrative arc
- Well-developed and intriguing characters
- Something in a character's history that motivates him
- Colorful, descriptions of settings, images, and culture
- Interesting, well-constructed sentence structure
- Smooth flow
- Intrigue, mystery, and curiosity
- Action, conflict, tension
- Inciting incidents
- Shocking twists and turns
- Upping the stakes throughout the story
- Compelling displays of emotions
- Logical unfolding of a plot
- Resolution satisfactory to the reader
- Distinctive voice of author without intruding on the story

The substantial nature of this list, which is in no way comprehensive, adds credence to the premise that good writers are in a state of continuous learning. Stephen King has said he is still learning. So did Gandhi. Let's learn about tools that support writing processes.

*Chapter 8*

# Writing Tools

*One only needs two tools in life: WD-40 to make things go, and duct tape to make them stop.*—G. M. Weilacher

A help desk child asked me if my cookies were activated. I was not going to tolerate trash talk from the Apple children. I responded, "Well, aren't you the little rascal." When he asked me to click on my browser, I didn't know what that was. I'm coming along, though. I know some stuff now, and I know that not all tools are worth fooling with.

Tools can be a blessing and a curse. Some are complicated beyond belief, others are expensive, and several are downright tricky. Spellcheck and auto-correct are examples of helpers who can turn into dicey traitors in an instant. Auto-correct is not always your friend. Don't be this lady who texted a guy friend, "I'll text you when I get to the restaurant." Her phone changed *text* to *sex*. He responded, "Hot damn!!!." If you are a seasoned writer, you know about writing tools. If you are an apprentice, listen up.

**TECHNOLOGY—THE WINDOW TO EVERYTHING:** An experienced writer knows one of the most notable challenges to producing a book is technology. It is also an extraordinary blessing. Mastering it is essential. The scope of digital influences on writing is too broad to cover in this book, but here are a couple of critical components.

**Search Engines:** With a computer or a cell phone, a writer possesses the most valuable tool imaginable. In just a couple of seconds he can look up words, spellings, grammar rules, formatting requirements, sentence structure principles, and stylistic guidelines. He can verify facts and explore unlimited information. Familiarize yourself with these portals to information and use the heck out of them. I Google my heart out when I'm writing. It is a tool extraordinaire.

**Backup:** Every experienced writer has a horror story about losing cherished work. Assure backup of manuscripts and related files. Some options include:

- email manuscripts to yourself or to someone else
- copy manuscripts to thumb drives
- take advantage of clouds
- use hard drive backup
- purchase a back-up service

I use all of these and Dropbox and iCloud (both are free). Google Drive is another popular cloud. Also, once I send a file to Amazon, another level of backup exists. Then there are, of course, hard copies if everything else fails. That sounds like an outlandish prospect at first blush, but in today's technological terrorist world, anything could happen.

**Graphic Design:** This is not for everyone, and unless you are interested in building out your orbit of capabilities, don't spend time on it. I tried it out and discovered I enjoyed it. My MacBook makes it easy. I've designed book covers, bookmarks, brochures, business cards, invitations to book-launch parties, and graphics for grandchildren. (They have business cards.) No one is more surprised at my being able to do all this than me.

I've learned, though, that book cover designers are inexpensive, and a professionally designed cover is better than anything I can produce. I recommend writers engage a professional to design covers. The cost runs around $150 to $300. Seek references from seasoned writers in your genre.

**Photos:** You can insert photos into books at no cost. I took training on photos at the Apple store and inserted them into my first memoir after which I asked, "Did I really do that?" In spite of considerable research, I never did figure out the dots per inch (DPI) requirement. It made me cry. Printers require 300 DPI, and they'll give you a hard time if your photos don't meet that standard. Having failed, I persuaded printers to accept photos that were not 300 DPI compliant and, in the final result, I couldn't tell the difference between those photos and the ones that complied. Go figure.

**POLISHING TOOLS:** The following tools require an author go over his manuscript many times. In his first book, these tools and exercises will reveal many opportunities for enhancement. As he inches toward *authorship*, many flaws will be avoided in the first place. He becomes an expert who can spot problems in his writing and that of others. This makes the writer an effective critique partner and coach. Here are polishing tools I use:

**Run-Throughs and Sweeps:** I suggest a writer go over and over his manuscript, each time focusing on specific editing or proofing requirements. The *run-through* and *sweep* processes outlined in the Appendix add layer after layer of polish. If these repetitive, revision process bother you, remember this: *Revision is writing.* These processes absolutely take writing to a higher level.

**Run-Throughs—Layering:** This involves going over and over the manuscript, each time focusing on specific objectives. Each run-through adds another layer of polish. Here are examples of run-through topics:

> select better words; add visually stimulating descriptions of settings, characters, and action; enhance emotions; add simile, metaphor, mantras, hooks, thought shots, spotlights; deepen development of characters and show growth; add dialogue; show—don't tell; strengthen voice; improve sentence structure

**Sweeps—Find and Fix:** This is a similar process except the writer goes through a book using the computer *find* capability to identify vulnerable areas and potential flaws. This is called *find and fix*. The process looks intimidating because there are so many potential problem areas. It would be a laborious task to check them all. But writers soon learn where their vulnerabilities lie, so they can direct trouble-shooting activities to those areas.

*Run-through—layering* topics and *sweeps—find and fix* opportunities are illustrated in detail in the Appendix.

**Reading for Perspective:** Read the draft over and over while viewing it from different perspectives: that of your audience, your most sensitive reader, other writers, and perhaps your mother and father. In my case, this is Aunt Weezie. My writing must surely frighten her at times and, in some circumstances, that tells me I'm on track. This process enhances sensitivity to others and assures the book speaks to its audience. Also, doing a read-through while pretending to be your harshest critic allows you to recast words in a way that makes it difficult for that person to criticize them.

**Multiple Drafts:** The more times a writer goes over his book the better it gets. Each draft delivers another level of polish. This is a never-ending process, and it is so productive that run-throughs become addictive. The writer knows if he does one more, the document will be better. How can he stop? At some point, he must stop, pull the trigger, and print, even knowing that one more time will make it better. I stopped counting iterations of drafts on my first book at sixty. Really. After ten years of writing, I've cut that in half.

The experience of every writer is different, of course, and I've had writers talk about three or four drafts. I question how they do that. I'd be ashamed of my fourth draft. If you are blessed with the capability to produce a polished book in just a few drafts, good for you. I would wonder, though, how much better it would be if you went through it more times.

**Spellcheck/Auto-Correct:** No doubt, as a writer, you've learned not to rely on spellcheck. It will not pick up everything. If you say *sour* instead of *soar, asses* instead of *assess, sweat* instead of *sweet, voluptuous* instead of *voluminous, tart* instead of *start, mustard* instead of *mustered, breath* instead of *breathe, isle* instead of *aisle, hart* instead of *heart,* or *pubic* instead of *public,* spellcheck is not going to catch it. Trust me. I know.

Also, word processing systems change words through auto-correct. Imagine my surprise during a run-through to see "some adverbs are *paragliding*" instead of "some adverbs are *palpable.*"

**REFERENCE BOOKS:** Most journalists and publishers follow the rules presented in the *Chicago Manual of Style*. The book is huge and expensive. A laminated cheatsheet of the manual is available through Amazon. Strunk and White's *The Elements of Style* is another generally accepted source of writing rules. An inexpensive, pocket-sized version is available on Amazon.

**A Thesaurus:** An online thesaurus is invaluable to writers for selecting just the right words—ones that are interesting, fascinating, and expressive—words that slaughter any possibility of a sentence being trite.

More specific word books are available. Angela Ackerman has a series of books that list word alternatives, including: *The Emotion Thesaurus, The Character Expression Thesaurus, The Negative Trait Thesaurus, The Positive Trait Thesaurus,* and *The Rural Setting Thesaurus.* Also, Barbara J. McMinn has a thesaurus of phrases. And I ran across a thesaurus for romance writers on Amazon but was so distracted by the erotic content that I can't recall the name of the author or her book. Sorry.

**PARTS OF A BOOK:** It seems strange to interpret book components as tools, but they are. Book structure is an instrument vital to book design, and many self-publishing writers misuse it by including too many of these parts in their books. (They also frequently misspell foreword and copyright). Agents and publishers marvel at such excesses, which can be the kiss of death to a submission.

---

### FRONT MATTER

**Title Page:** Includes title, subtitle, and author. (Information should match verbiage on the book cover.)

**Publisher Page:** On the back of the Title Page, this includes copyright, Library of Congress notice, publication info, ISBN, legal notices, and credits for production, photography, editing, and illustration.

**Dedication:** (Optional)

**Acknowledgments:** (Optional) Author expresses gratitude for those contributing to the book and those supporting him through the process. (This can be in back matter.)

**Epigraph:** (Optional) Quote or short comment commonly placed on left page facing the Table of Contents. Epigraphs are also used after chapter titles.

**Table of Contents:** Lists divisions, chapters, and enough detail that readers can navigate the book.

**Foreword:** (Optional) Written by someone other than the author and signed and dated. Provides context for the book. Spell correctly (not foreward, forward, or forword).

**Preface:** (Optional) Written by the author. Tells how the book came into being and provides background information, although this can be included in the Introduction.

**Introduction:** Author explains purpose and goals of the book, places it in context, declares disclosures, and spells out scope and organization. Don't start the story in the Introduction.

**Prologue:** (Optional) In fiction, this sets the scene. It is told in the voice of a character or narrator (not the author).

## BODY

**Section Break Pages:** Similar to acts of a play, a book can be divided into Sections or Parts presented on a book's right-side page with odd page numbers.

**Chapter Pages:** A chapter can begin with a title, subtitle, and epigraph (optional quote) presented on right-side page with odd page numbers. Put no page numbers on blank pages.

**Epilogue:** (Optional) An ending piece (in the voice of the author or a character) meant to tidy up the ending, bring closure, and/or to bring the reader up to date.

## BACK MATTER

**Appendix:** Informative details and helpful tools:

> **Index:** Alphabetical listing of words used throughout the book with associated page numbers
>
> **Glossary:** Alphabetical list of terms defined
>
> **Bibliography:** References
>
> **Books by Author:** List with short descriptions
>
> **About the Author:** Biography

---

Don't overload readers with front matter or back matter. Some can be combined into one page, such as *Acknowledgment* and *Dedication. Preface* and *Introduction* can be redundant if both are used. Prologues are out of favor with many agents and publishers.

**PONDERING AS A TOOL:** Another activity that is so advantageous it qualifies as a tool is pondering, the process of concentrating. This is how a writer searches his mind and comes up with ideas or better words. Too often writers write, write, write. Even if they sense a glitch, the momentum carries them on. Perfect a knack for spotting glitches and doing something about them. I love it when I see workshop participants stare. They are going to make something better.

Exercising induces pondering on steroids. When a workout frees the mind and sends blood flowing to the brain, solutions pop up spontaneously. If you get stuck, go for a walk or work out. Take a pen and paper or a phone with you. It's going to rain ideas.

When you hit a wall that craft and tools can't bust through, seek out other writers and slide in sideways. Let's learn how to make the most of writer collaboration.

*Chapter 9*

# Collaborators

*Criticism is hard to take. The ego is fragile. But feedback is frosting. Seek it out. Eat it up. Just know that some critics are assholes.*

Writing is a lonely profession. Writers peck away on computers in isolated places and in cubbyholes in their homes where submission reject letters burst from files or cover the walls. Storyboards plastered with plot lines, messy notebooks, overflowing files, stacks of books, computers covered with sticky notes, and chair seats topped with pillows clutter the decor.

Writers are vagrants, lingering with noice-cancelling headphones in libraries, coffee shops, and cafes. Like moles, they seal themselves away in remote writers' colonies, solitary beach houses, and secluded log-cabin retreats. As wanderers, they ply their trade in airports, hotels, planes, campsites, and hospital waiting rooms. At family reunions they can be found in Aunt Maude's guest room pecking away while the laughter of relatives frolicking in the living room rocks the house.

It is against their nature to commune, even with fellow writers. Who needs colleagues when a book-in-process flaunts a plot rich with urgency and mystique? Every writer does.

**COLLEAGUES—THE FORCE:** The single most important thing new writers should do is to become part of the writer community. The complexities and demands of the writing profession are articulated throughout this book, but most issues writers wrestle with have been solved by other writers. Tapping into that is critical if *authorship* is to be achieved. Successful writers collaborate with comrades, those with common spirits who champion their work.

**Writers' Groups:** I believe the most important and urgent thing a new writer should do is join a writers' group. Rookies need access to advice and resources to efficiently master craft and access services. Seasoned writers in these groups support the efforts of others and keep novices out of trouble and the clutches of scammers and opportunists. The publishing industry is a minefield for naive writers.

**Writers' Conferences:** These provide exceptional travel experiences, bountiful learning opportunities, occasions to commune with other writers, and the prospect of networking with important people.

**Workshops:** These are typically intense and demanding learning experiences, rich with critique and writing demands. Most formats require a writer open himself up to criticism. In Bill Bernhardt's workshops, writers are expected to deliver a chapter a day for critique by him and at least six other writers in the group. The breakthroughs I've experienced in workshop settings have yielded sweeping consequences. Such venues represent the epitome of collaboration.

**Classes:** A serious writer will take college writing courses. Fortunately, most educational institutions have adult programs tailored to older writers. Often regular classes can be audited for free, which allows writers to mingle with young, exuberant college students—an enlightening and inspiring experience. These courses offer a rare opportunity to connect with professors who can open doors and give good counsel. Most are generous with sharing personal career-path experiences and with helping students to enhance theirs.

**Critique Groups:** John Osborne said, "Asking a writer what he thinks about criticism is like asking a lamppost what it feels about dogs." Critique is hard to take, and the more valid, the tougher it is to accept. However, it is an incubator for the evolution of a story, and it just might keep a writer out of trouble. My critique group saved me:

> In a book on aging I developed for a workshop for seniors at a university lifelong learning program, I worked hard to keep this tough subject upbeat and positive. However, in the Introduction, while making a case for why the book was important, I exposed the downsides of aging in the first few paragraphs. My critique group said this was a downer and would discourage buyers. They said, "Who would want to read about such a depressing topic?"

> How could I have missed that? I was so concerned with explaining why the book was necessary that I ensured no one would want to read it. I had massacred the book's upbeat message of how to age in a way that is a gift to others.

It takes the right blend of people to make a critique group effective. A small group of writers in the same genre is usually best. So is a group with seasoned writers. One made up entirely of novices will struggle. Search online for "critique group processes" and study up, so you can be an effective participant. Critique cuts deeply, and not all of it is good advice. But the potential for enhancing outcomes is profound. Ideally, the book should be well developed before you seek critique.

Don't create your story and then stick to it. You didn't birth it. It's just a story. Be cautious about ardent defense of your position on why or how you wrote what you did. The critics might be right. If they didn't "get it," your readers may not either, and you won't be around to explain it to them. Don't argue with feedback, just accept it or not. It's your call.

Workshops are an excellent source for critique by other writers. Both the Iowa Writers' Festival and Bill Bernhardt's workshops have been valuable critique sources for me. Many famous authors offer workshops. It is best to seek out one in your genre; however, let me qualify that. I've been the only nonfiction writer in a couple of workshops, and I learned a lot from the fiction writers. I believe they learned from me.

**Beta Readers:** This is a higher level review than editing. It is typically performed by a seasoned writer and focuses on the construct of the story and the effectiveness of the writing rather than proofreading. Therefore, it is done when the manuscript is fully developed or possibly in the galley copy stage (final proofing from a bound book).

A writer must integrate himself into the writer community to have access to effective beta readers. Tapping into readers who specialize in the same genre is best. Reading your book and giving input is a generous act. Thank beta readers profusely. Some who commit to doing so never get around to it, or they take so long you've got the book out before they get back to you. Paying them and setting a completion date helps. I've been paid $100 for such reads.

These experts might be supplemented with a friend or two as beta readers. The problem is that they are going to love, love, love what you wrote. So give them a list of questions. For example:

- What is the strongest chapter?
- What is the weakest chapter?
- What was your favorite part? Your least favorite?
- If I had to take a chapter out, which would you recommend?
- Is there anything that confused you—needs more explanation?
- Is there anything not believable or that didn't make sense?
- Was there any portion you wanted to skip?
- What was your impression of the chapter sizes?
- Did you like the titles?
- Were the settings appropriate and visually portrayed?
- Did you like the characters? Were they believable?
- To write a three-sentence review, what would you say?

This may or may not work. Most likely, these friendly reviewers will still love, love, love what you wrote.

**Your Editor as Wingman:** For purposes of this chapter and the next one, the editor is an editor/ proofreader (as apposed to a publishing company editor who recruits and manages writers). Although the writer/ editor relationship is professional and usually at arm's length, collaborate closely with your editor. Make her your wingman. Persuade her to teach you reasons behind suggested edits. Learn everything she knows. Nothing moves an apprentice writer faster along the continuum of learning than sitting with an editor and going over edits, item by item.

How do you find an editor? Join a writers' group. How much does an editor cost? What they charge is all over the place. Two dollars a page is a benchmark. You might find a good one who won't let you pay them, in which case I suggest a gift certificate. Whatever one costs, it might be the best money you ever spent as an author.

**THE IMPERTINENCE OF CRITIQUE:** The last thing you need is a timid, kindly person critiquing your work. You need a tough old bird like me. There's no easy way for an editor to point out errors and problems, especially when the writer is new and there are many of them. You must buck up and take your licks. Don't be like this character in Orson Scott Card's book, *Alvin Journeyman*:

> And if you're going to criticize me for not finishing the whole thing and tying it up in a bow for you, why, do us both a favor and write your own damn book, only have the decency to call it a romance instead of a history, because history's got no bows on it, only frayed ends of ribbons and knots that can't be untied. It ain't a pretty package, but then, it's not your birthday, that I know of, so I'm under no obligation to give you a gift.

In general, it is not a good idea to respond to critical reviews, especially on the Internet. Doing so can lead to a cat fight, like so many interactions on social media. Writers are under no obligation to "sell" their positions to anyone, but it is prudent to remain openminded and consider that a critic might be right. On the other hand, a "thank you" for a good review would surely be appreciated and might help build a writer's following.

Editing details in the next chapter explain why most writers spend a couple of years getting a book out. Editing can be a pain, but flirt with it. Teaming up with an expert editor and learning from her is potent support.

## Chapter 10

## Editing—The Polish, The Shine

*I can't write five words but that I change seven*—Dorothy Parker

Finding an error in an already published book is akin to discovering a tarantula in the bathtub. And every writer has had that experience. Why? Because the alphabet consists of 26 letters from which a writer creates a 100,000-word, 300-page book. That, my dear writers, is the universe showing off. It also explains why it is impossible to create the perfect book. But you should try.

For me, proofreading is the most tedious, challenging, and frustrating part of producing a book, other than technology. I eventually licked the technology issue—sort of. I didn't win in the proofing arena. I found errors in all my books after publication. I've never nailed the editing, and that makes me feel like a special kind of stupid.

When I plan out a timeline for producing a book, I consider the time required for editing and double it. I had three people edit my last book. Each found valid but different mistakes. When I read it one last time, I found six more. After it was published, I found three more. I'm certain if I read it again, I'd find more. Thanks to print on demand, these errors were corrected and a revised electronic file submitted before the next book was printed. Salvation.

Editing and proofing are often used interchangeably, and the difference between them is blurred. Technically, editing is broader than proofing and usually encompasses rewriting and restructuring as well as some proofing. Proofreading, often called line-editing, is focused more on grammar, spelling, punctuation, sentence structure, and formatting. Most writers I know have one person do both editing and proofing.

The editing definition is further complicated by publishing companies who have editors, people serving as scouts who seek out writers to nurture through the process of publication. The context for *editor* in this chapter is limited to editor/ proofreaders who are reviewing books for authors before they are printed or submitted to agents or publishers.

**SEEKING PERFECTION:** Editing is the bane of most authors' writing experiences. If you are determined to re-read until you find no errors, good luck with that. It never happens. You will find errors, or at least needed improvements, every time. Most likely, you will never produce the perfect book, but set that as a goal anyway.

Whether you take time to do all the steps proposed here is a personal choice. Know that even if you do them all, perfection will elude you. When you find an imperfection in something already published, give thanks for print on demand, which allows you to fix mistakes before the next book is printed. And consider this coping tactic: a well-timed, "Oh, well."

**SELF-EDITS:** Normally, a book is produced in two phases, each with a different format: the *manuscript format* and the *book format*. This is explained in *Chapter 12 - Printing*. The major differences between the two formats is that *manuscript* is on 8 1/2 x 11, double spaced, front side only. *Book format* is usually 6 x 9, single spaced, two-sided. Under the traditional publishing model, writers deliver the manuscript format to the publisher and they edit and reformat to the book format for printing.

A self-publisher is responsible for editing the manuscript and reformatting it to the book format. I skip the manuscript format and write directly into book format, which eliminates this conversion process. It requires my editors be okay with editing from book format. Many editors are not. They want double-spacing, which provides more space to make notes.

I do self-edits before delivering a book to my editors so it is as clean as I can get it. I do a *format edit* separate from a *text edit* because the editing process is different for each. Following are checklists for these edits:

---

### Self Edit - "Format" Checklist
(Some of these are not applicable to the manuscript format.)
**Check Setup:**
- Margins and Margin Justification
- Header Footer Locations
- Section Breaks

**Check Chapters:**
- Section Breaks/Page Breaks
- Chapters Start on Odd Page Number (Right side)
- No Header on First Page of Chapters
- Chapter Numbers/Titles Correct
- Chapter Number/Titles Tied to Table of Contents
- Chapter Number/Titles Tied to Chapter Headers
- Subtitles Correct
- Spacing Down to Each Chapter Title Consistent
- Spacing Between Title/Sub-titles/Text Consistent
- Font Size Consistent in Chapter Titles/Subtitles

**Check Headers/Footers:**
- Chapter Numbers and Titles Correct
- Font Size/Style Consistent
- No Headers on Blank Pages

**Check Page Numbers:**
- Flow Properly Throughout
- All Numbers Located in Same Spot on Page
- No Page Numbers on Blank Pages

**Check Indents:**
- Paragraphs and any Indented Text

**Check Table of Contents:**
- Verify Page Numbers (odd numbers for chapter heads)
- Table of Contents Titles/Numbers Match Chapter/Headers

**Verify Index Page Numbers**

---

For the text edit, I proofread over and over until there are few errors found. Then I do the following:

## Self-Edit - "Text" Checklist

Zoom in. Read word-by-word on computer. Read out loud from a hard copy:

- Verify Dates, Numbers, Proper Names, Cross References
- Verify Quotation Marks and Parentheses Are Paired
- Assure No Widows (single word on a line at end of paragraph; short paragraph on page at end of chapter; single line of a paragraph at beginning or end of page)
- Check for Parallel Structure in Series of Words or Phrases
- Look for Unintentional Font Size or Style Changes
- Check for Single Spacing at End of Sentences
- Verify Questions End with Question Marks
- Verify Periods and Commas Are Inside Quotes
- Assure Paragraphs Have Ending Punctuation (missing period at end of paragraph is a common error)
- Verify Consistent Use of Capitalization and Punctuation on Lists and Headings

**Important:** When making corrections, double check them. Re-read twice the entire paragraph in which a change was made. Yes, twice. Check the influence of that change on page numbers, chapter breaks, Table of Contents, and Index.

---

**Editing Tips:** The buck stops with the writer. To be taken seriously, he must deliver a polished manuscript to an agent or publisher. A self-publishing author must take part in both the manuscript edit and the book edit stages. If he does not, he is unlikely to produce a quality product. Additionally, editing expertise is a crucial step on the road to *authorship*. Here are tips that will make you a better self-editor:

- Put the manuscript aside for a week or so between writing and proofing.
- Proof from hard copy. Read slowly and out loud. Don't mumble. Pretend you're reading to an audience. You'll hear mistakes. Allow several days to do this so you don't lose your voice.
- Zoom in and proof on the computer word by word.
- Be brutal about trimming. It will make the piece richer, stronger, and tighter.
- At some point, read from the perspective of your harshest critic. This results in tweaks that make a difference in content and tone and removes ammunition they could use to criticize.
- Proofread only when you are mentally alert. If you are not finding mistakes, you may be tired and missing them. Take a break.
- Don't always review from front to back. Mix it up. Read complicated chapters first when you are fresh or start from the last chapter and work backward.
- Proof everything. Don't ignore page numbers, headers, footers, chapter titles, etc.

**A FRESH SET OF EYES:** No matter how much self-editing is done, it is necessary to have someone else proof your work. A fresh set of eyes will spot errors you missed, regardless of how proficient you are.

Trust your judgment on whether to take the advice of editors. Some suggestions are subjective. My editors disagree over use of the word "that." One takes them out. The other puts them in. I value both perspectives and, as a result, I find a nice balance. When there is controversy, pick a method and be consistent in its application.

**HOW TO GET THE ALMOST PERFECT BOOK:** I say "almost" because it is unlikely you will produce a perfect book. Proofreading skills can be learned. It will take awhile to master editing, but slow and steady progress will turn you into a pro. An intense sense of accomplishment results from learning the skills required to be good at editing. Not even the best editor does a perfect job, so don't be intimidated.

I use five stages of editing and allow at least three months for the process. The goal is to produce the perfect book. (I have never met that goal.):

> **Stage I: Self-Edit -** This is the editing process I described above. I have this grand illusion I'm going to impress my editors, but they find plenty of errors. It's humbling. Still, my goal is to deliver a polished product. So I review the book over and over with the goal of finding no errors. Since that never happens, after about ten iterations, I surrender.
>
> **Stage II: Beta Readers -** Through KDP Amazon (my printer), I transform the book's file into a bound proof book (called *galley copy* in the industry). I order several copies and ask seasoned writers and friends to do a beta read. This is a higher level review than proofreading. I'm looking for input on writing technique, what works and what does not, as well as obvious errors. (I sometimes use select comments from beta readers as reviews—with their consent, of course.)
>
> **Stage III: Edit/Proofing -** While the beta-reader review is happening, I give a bound proof book to all three of my editors. (Most writers give their books to editors in manuscript format. I don't.*) Each editor has a different background and each one finds different things. And I do another edit myself while waiting for their input. The results of all these edits and beta reviews are installed and double checked for

accuracy. I then order a corrected proof. (One of my editors volunteers to check out the changes.)

**Stage IV: Final Edit** - I review both the cover and the text one last time. Again, it is critical to proof format and text separately. (The proofing processes are different for each.) I brace myself because I know I will find errors even after all that editing. Fixes are made and double checked.

**Stage V:** Once the book is live on Amazon, I order a copy through them to test out the reader experience. I sit curled up on the sofa and read it as though I am a reader—for pleasure. Guess what. I find errors, usually several. For this reason, I don't announce the book or schedule a launch until I've had time to do this final, post-publication process and send Amazon a revised file.

---

*Note: I write my books in the format for 6 x 9 book printing. If you are writing in manuscript format, you will not have a bound proof copy for Steps II and III.

These details on my editing process explain why I allow at least three months for editing. The first month is me editing. The second is my editors and beta readers doing it. The third is spent fixing and double checking.

Susan Bell alluded to the importance of the editing process in *The Artful Edit*. She said, "Write into the void. . .edit into the universe." A winsome thought, this suggests editing is somehow important in the grand scheme of things. I don't know about the universal influences, but I do know that after three months of editing I'm sick to death of my book. I get over this quickly, though, when I see it on Amazon and hold a copy in my hands. It's a beauty.

**FIXING PUBLISHED ERRORS:** When an imperfection is discovered in something already submitted or published, be grateful for print on demand and console yourself with this thought: *Errors are the hand of man.* Apply the coping tactic mentioned earlier, a well-timed "Oh, well."

If you self-publish through a print-on-demand vendor, you can most likely send in a corrected file at any time and the next book printed will include those fixes. If you use Amazon's KDP to print and Amazon to sell, you can submit a revised file for free. The book might be unavailable on Amazon for a few days while the corrected file is loaded.

> **HINT:** When ordering books, order only as many as you need immediately, so you don't end up with a large inventory of books with errors in them. Thirty such books, not so bad. A hundred, not good.

We writers are in this together, and all of us are having the same experiences. When I find errors in books of writers I know, I send them an email asking whether they want input. I love it when writers do the same for me. Some writers create new files and fix errors. Others are on to other things. If they respond positively, I send them the information in an email. I stick to obvious typos and stay away from any controversial or gray areas.

**FLAWS AS PATINA:** Editing is just damage control. A writer is unlikely to achieve perfection. But go for the perfect book and get as close to it as you can. Consider imperfections as patina, something similar to the green on aged copper that many consider beautiful. The important thing is that you created something. In doing so, you give a gift, one that will last for generations. Celebrate. Be like the crazy-ass character in one of my stories who said to his friend who had done something incredible, "That's stupid wonderful. Makes me feel so pedestrian. Let's go get you a tattoo."

# SECTION III

Memoir and Contests—Paths to
Joy and Purpose

*When you capture a life story (yours or someone else's), relatives develop a sense of their heritage. Descendants will do the same years from now. They may never experience the time and place where their ancestor grew up, but they will know that time and place. They may never meet the persons whose stories you told, but they will know them. When you write memoir, you create legacy, and legacies are forever.*

*Chapter 11*

# About Memoir

*Wow! Grandma Is Way Cooler Than I Thought.*

A man in awe of a fascinating journal he had written years ago said, "If I had known it was that interesting, I would have written more." This illustrates the magic of memoir. Life stories are treasures. I've written two memoirs: the first for family and the second for girlfriends, which included the juicy details left out of the first one. I was frustrated while writing the first one and joyful when writing the second one five years later. The reason? I had learned to focus on the aspects of writing that made me happy and to write whatever the hell I wanted.

**MEMOIR DEFINED:** When teaching memoir-writing classes, one of the most common questions I'm asked is, "What is the difference between biography and memoir?" The differences are fuzzy, but in general, biography is a chronological, comprehensive, fact-based account of an entire life. Memoir is story-like and encompasses only certain aspects of a life. Biography is written by someone other than who it is about, unless it's an autobiography. Memoir is usually written by the person it is about.

Here is what memoir is not: It is not diary scrawl or a journal. Neither is it a preachy conversion tool, at least it shouldn't be. (That would be an essay or an inspirational book.) It is not about bragging, venting, therapy, retaliation, right-fighting, factual drool, glorification, or fiction.

What memoir is about is seeking answers, self-discovery, sharing of wisdom, and recording a life story. Memoir is a quest—a life review, which involves unfolding, interpreting, and filling in the blanks. Memoir is about discovering the essence of a person and creating legacy. This is important because legacies are forever.

Memoir writers run the gamut from professional authors to people who've never written before.

> When it comes to memoir, a technically flawed life story has an endearing charm all its own. Do not be intimidated by the task. You are capturing a life story and creating the gift of legacy. What is more worthwhile than that? It is not important that you have the perfect book. It is just important that you have one. As I've said before, memoir trumps craft.

Many memoirs are written by professional writers or famous people who have resources to polish their work. With big publishers behind them, they have a shot at becoming a best seller. However, most memoirs are written by amateur writers about unknown people. No matter how wonderful these books are, they nestle into anonymity with sales not breaking the average of 250. And that's okay. They exist, and they are a gift to those close to the life that was chronicled. Memoir is not about book sales. Memoir is not about money. Memoir is about life.

**Why Write a Life Story?** Through memoir, the past connects with the future and generations link together in a common thread. History and wisdom that would otherwise be lost forever are preserved. Capturing a life story is investing in others. It is a love letter to children, grandkids, siblings, nieces and nephews, future generations, and those who love the person whose life is recorded.

**A Life Review:** Writing a memoir serves as a canvas for discovery because it requires a life review, a process that shines a fresh light on the past. The writer discovers she did the best she could with what she knew and what she had, and others did the same.

With adult eyes, she sees herself as a vulnerable, innocent child. She marvels at the grit and fortitude of that child and falls in love with her and the adult she became. Self-esteem blossoms. Acceptance cradles her spirit. Her view of parents and other adults is enhanced because she has now played those roles and can comprehend the challenges they entail. With that clarity, the sacrifices others made for her become apparent—forgiveness beckons and gratefulness flourishes. How about that? A good reason to write a memoir, huh?

**Obstacles to Writing a Life Story:** Unless you're a writer, documenting a life story is an intimidating task, one that requires courage and fortitude. You might say:

"I can't write." The truth is: Everyone can write. Be bold. You can do it.

"My life is not interesting." The truth is: Yes, it is. It absolutely is. Everyone's life is fascinating.

"It's egotistical to write about myself." The truth is: It is not. Every life is worthy of capture.

"I'll have more time to do it later." The truth is: maybe —maybe not. Look around.

In my book *Capture Life—Write a Memoir*, I show how to overcome these objections. Be prideful about whatever delightfully flawed narrative you produce. Know you are creating something that will live for generations. Legacy.

**THE NUANCES OF MEMOIR:** You can do it. You can write your life story or someone else's. Writing memoir is messy business, though. Here is how to get started and how to stay out of trouble.

**Frame of Reference:** Before you put pen to paper, contemplate your reason for chronicling a life. With your audience in mind, consider what you want to achieve. Do you want to entertain, share wisdom, record historical details, inspire young people, show how to age well, prove that Grandma was way cooler than anyone thought, or all these things? What do you want readers to take away? This information determines the frame of reference from which you write. Keep it in mind throughout the process. It influences the tone of the writing.

**Tone:** This reflects the overall spirit of a book. It is communicated by what is included, what is left out, and how things are said. There are plenty of examples of famous people pressured by publishers to reveal hurtful and embarrassing information in the interest of creating a provocative memoir that sells. Don't do that.

It is said in the publishing industry that to be interesting, a writer must be willing to kill his own grandmother. A more sensitive but stranger saying is that there are some things you shouldn't write about until your parents are dead. Whatever you do, be nice. Don't be indiscriminate and insensitive about what you write about and how you say it. An unpleasant situation can be made gentle with the right words. Tantalizing revelations are not going to help your book sell— unless you are a movie star or a politician. Fascinating information masterfully conveyed with sensitivity might not sell either, but your integrity will be intact.

A memoirist is wise to remember not everyone's story is his to tell. When assessing the impact of what you write about another person, pretend you are that person while reading it out loud. This will guide you into sensitive territory. And remember this: *If you hurt someone with words, you hurt everyone around them.*

**Theme:** People are complex, and everyone's life has several themes, which are revealed in the first draft process described in the next chapter. A writer is wise to select a prevailing theme, set it up in the first chapter, touch on it occasionally throughout the book (don't overdo), and nail the meaning of it in the last chapter.

A theme reflects a person's way of being in the world— the frame of reference from which they operate. These questions reveal themes: What makes you shine? What are you afraid of? How do you respond to crisis? What or whom do you gravitate to? What or whom do you avoid? Why? What makes you cry? What gives you joy?

Themes define a person. One is a consummate rescuer committed to serving others. Another repeatedly sabotages things when life is good. A person may be a bold and fearless risk taker who jumps out of airplanes, drives like a raving idiot, and listens to Led Zeppelin while showering. Another volunteers, rescues animals, and paints clowns. Often people are not aware of behavioral patterns or the themes behind them. Memoir brings them to light and creates self-awareness. Themes are revealed by studying patterns of behavior. They are fodder for an enticing memoir.

An eternal optimist who finds the good in everyone and everything and occasionally gets "had" is going to have a different theme from a shrewd manipulator and opportunist. A high-energy character who sees life as a party going on will have an upbeat theme, while a church lady's theme will be more staid—maybe. People who surround themselves with musicians, artists, and puppies present a different theme from those who commune with wrestlers, bikers, and hunters. This variation in characters is a writer's smorgasbord.

Several sub-themes may be included in a memoir by incorporating them in stories and chapters. These minor themes make great chapter titles. Explore ways to make them fit under the umbrella of the major theme. Don't overdo the major theme. It does not have to be articulated in every chapter, and it should not intrude on the stories. Hint at it and readers will figure it out.

**The Order of Things:** Structure involves stringing stories and chapters together in a logical fashion. A memoir does not have to be in chronological order. In fact, that can be less interesting than one in which chapters are determined by themes, events, persons, messages, or whatever. Be creative. No right or wrong ways exist to structure a life story—only interesting ones.

**FINDING THE TRUTH**: When a memoirist writes something, readers expect it to be true, but is it? Is faulty memory lying? Finding the truth is not a tidy business. Memoir writing is about the illusion of truth. Memories are determined by the point of view of the person recalling them.

Each person has his own interpretation of events. It is not unusual for siblings to ask, "Did we have the same parents?" The first born has a different experience than the last one. I was financially strapped while raising my older child and affluent while raising the younger one. Their experiences were significantly dissimilar.

Also, when people recall the past, they reconstruct it. This results in wildly different recollections. Understanding how others view the past and acknowledging their interpretations in a memoir can add interest and lead to healing differences.

Then there is the issue of dialogue. No one can recall the exact words said, but it is generally acceptable to create accurate, though not necessarily verbatim, conversations in order to tell a story. Dialogue—usually in short, efficient doses—enhances a memoir by bringing characters to life.

A memoirist must write his story in his own way, based on his point of view. Some go so far as to create composite characters, change names and other details, and even compress multiple incidents into one. These adjustments to history are usually done to protect the identity of characters. Memoir purists oppose such actions, but the trend is toward general acceptance of them as long as the writer lets readers know what they have done, usually in the form of a disclosure in the Introduction.

It is acceptable to include family folklore in memoir as long as it is labeled as such. Adventuresome writers can explore the relatively new genre of creative nonfiction, a blend of fiction and fact. It is flexible and takes memoir writing to a high level of reconstruction. Ohio University's director of creative writing, Dinty W. Moore, talks about this genre in his book, *Crafting the Personal Essay: A guide to Writing and Publishing Creative Nonfiction.*

Everyone has their own truth, but you are the author. Your memories rule. (Read Tracy Seeley's book *Truth in Memoir*.)

**Victim Mentality:** Evaluate the state of mind from which you write. Any memoirist can find reasons to assume a victim role and weave a tone of persecution and abuse into a life story. If your goal is to dish out paybacks by writing your story, you may need to consult an attorney before publishing the book. Revenge writing can be problematic. A better and more productive approach is to write about how you and others overcame the harsh realities of life.

Consider Frank McCourt's *Angela's Ashes*. In spite of a nightmarish childhood, which he was fortunate to survive, he managed to make tremendously flawed parents sympathetic characters. His work stands as a tonic for other damaged children and as a cathartic remedy for parents who were the casualty of their own misfortunes. Janet Walls did the same in her memoir *The Glass Castle*. Both memoirs were made into movies and are must reads for anyone aspiring to write their life story.

Consider this: Most people did the best they could with what they had and what they knew. Soften the edges of hurts. Consider the tragedies in people's lives that made them who they are and caused them to do what they did. At some point in your life, you were, no doubt, an abuser. People are flawed. There are no perfect parents. Before you harshly criticize someone, look into your own past behavior.

Don't ignore the mistakes of others and the hurts and vulnerabilities they produced if such experiences are relevant. But focus on how you overcame them rather than wallowing in misery for having experienced them. By doing so, you paint inspirational pictures of how it is possible to rise above the anguish of the past. Those triumphs are gifts to readers.

When I was a senior in high school, I begged to go to college. My dad said, "I can't send you to college. I have four boys to educate." I could have carried the unfairness of that around for years and played it out raw in my memoir. But I understood the culture he came from. And I understood why my response at that time was acceptance. We were both victims in a way. I told about this incident in my memoir because it was an important reflection of the time, but I did not go into victim mode and criticize my father's words. I defended him.

**Omissions:** A memoir is not a comprehensive biographical account. It is a compilation of select stories. You get to choose what to put in and what to leave out. Omissions are okay. Not everything you know about others is fair game. Some stories are not yours to tell. But be bold where you can about including unfortunate incidents and behaviors that define a life and offer important messages. Take accountability for your actions when you contributed to problems or caused negative consequences.

**WRITING THE BAD:** In general, write your truth your way. If someone doesn't like what you wrote, they can write their own damn book. Anne Lamott said: "If people wanted you to write more warmly about them, they should have behaved better."

> I wrote a nonfiction piece about cowboys. They were a reckless, wooly bunch. I was tough on them because a writing instructor who critiqued an early draft suggested I was too gentle. She said, "I wanted so badly for you to call them out on their bad behavior." So I did, but I interjected considerable humor. This changed the tone, and the cowboys loved it. The piece won First Place in a contest.

Life is not always a civilized business. A Pollyanna piece would be boring. An honest story replete with flawed characters and missteps demonstrates to readers the realities of life. It's not so much about what happened as it is about how you or someone else overcame adversity and what was learned from the experience.

Mistakes and lessons learned have the potential to become an antibiotic for a foolish mistake over which a reader is agonizing. Through your life story, you become the voice of reason to a young person you care about who is feeling guilty about something or hovering on the cusp of a bad decision—even generations from now. How important is that?

When viewing toxic adults as hurt children, a sense of compassion surfaces. A skillful writer can portray ugliness with delicacy and imply the obvious without stating it. For example: In a memoir, a woman implied abuse by her husband without exposing information detrimental to their children. She said, "And then his hateful words turned into action." Nothing more needed to be said. (Read *Handling the Truth—On Writing of Memoir* by Beth Kephart)

**Protecting Identities:** Some stories that cry out to be told would be hugely embarrassing or even damaging to a person. Ways around this include changing names, places, and other details so, supposedly, readers cannot tell who the story is about. There are two problems with this approach. It often doesn't work, and the result is fiction. Writers can turn memoirs into fiction books, and that's fine. In a memoir, though, fiction is not appropriate. The writing community has alleviated this problem to some extent with the genre of creative nonfiction, which has become popular. Study it if you decide to embrace that approach to a life story. It's a touchy task.

Another technique for hiding identities is to develop composite characters in whom the attributes of two or more people are combined. Memoir purists disapprove of this, but I did it in *Red Heels and Smokin'* in a chapter about three Oklahoma rednecks I had dated. The stories were true, but the characters were a blend of three men. It was as though I put them together in a sack, shook them up, and new characters showed up with different names. I did this to protect their identities, which turned out to be unnecessary. Little did I know at the time how proud rednecks were of their bad behavior and the delight they would take in the redneck, macho, shitheads label I gave them. If you tinker with identities, as I did, disclose your actions.

**Historical Connections and Influences:** Writing about life's events by intersecting them with historical ones makes a story more interesting and provides context for readers. Portray experiences as history lessons, but know it is not the historical events that are the heart of these stories. It is the emotional responses to them. Focus on those.

It is not the cold war that is significant to a memoir. It is the fear it elicited. It is not the Vietnam war that is the heart of a life story, it's the grip it still has on a veteran's psyche. It is the brotherhood, the losses, the killing, the fungus, the music, the smells, the drug addiction that still owns him, the shrapnel he carries in his body, and the nightmares that torture his sleep to this day. It's why he hits the floor in a tire shop all these years later when someone drops a tire rim. Take historical events to an emotional level and explore the consequences they provoke.

**Biases and Opinions:** The objective of memoir is to share life stories, not to soapbox or convert readers to the writer's opinions. There is a fine line between sharing wisdom and being preachy. Consider this: Just because you think something in your head does not make it true. It is a thought. Hold your opinions softly. When they overwhelm a memoir, readers with different opinions are turned off. This could be someone important in your life, such as a grandchild with whom you want to share your story. Readers don't sign up for reading a memoir to be converted. If you want to write a manifesto, do so, but that is not memoir.

**WHAT'S IN IT FOR YOU:** After having written a memoir, you will know:

> You won't die with your story still in you, and you will have given the gift of legacy.

**Selling Memoir:** Memoir writers often harbor illusions of a best seller, but thousands of memoirs are produced every year, and the market is saturated. Many don't have universal appeal or are about a fall of some sort followed by the road to recovery. Publishers are looking for something fresh.

An author should consider their book successful if fifty friends and family members purchase it, or if nieces and nephews want to sit at her table at a family reunion, or if grandchildren are convinced grandma is way cooler than they thought, or if she reconnected with a high school friend who read the book. One memoirist described success this way: "People are still talking to me, at least those I care about."

When it comes to memoir, sales is not a valid measure of success. When you capture a life story (yours or someone else's), relatives develop a sense of their heritage. Descendants will do the same years from now. They may never experience the time and place where their ancestor grew up, but they will know that time and place. They may never meet the persons whose stories you told, but they will know them. Documented stories live forever. Frame your definition of success as a writer around that scenario, and you will be successful indeed.

Imagine generations from now an ancestor finding your memoir in an attic. No doubt, he will marvel at this find, study the cover, flip through the pages, touch the photos, and say out loud, "Wow!"

*Chapter 12*

# Writing Memoir

*I'm not egocentric enough to think I'm so interesting that someone would want to tap my phone or otherwise spy on me. In fact, my only hope of getting stalked is at a car lot or a furniture store.*

Writing about yourself is egocentric. This is why some writers call the first draft of a memoir vomiting onto paper. Randy Travis would call it digging up bones. Perhaps a better label for the first draft is: a mechanism for discovering the essence of a life.

**THE CRAFT OF WRITING MEMOIR:** Writers spend years studying their craft. How deep a memoir writer gets into this is a personal choice. He doesn't have to be an expert. It can be rewarding, though, to embark on a learning journey. Understanding the basic concepts of writing will enhance the product. One way to do this is to read memoirs written by experts. (See Appendix for recommended readings)

Reading these experts will be humbling because most likely you, like me, cannot hope to match their talent. But you can do your own thing. You can write, and your noble efforts will count for something. You don't have to build a Cadillac. A shiny Kia will do nicely. You are never going to have the perfect book. The important thing is that you have one.

**Memoir As a Story:** Someone, I don't know who, said, *"Shit happens* is not a story." That's a crude way of making a point, but it is valid. Just telling about yourself, others, and events in your life is not a story. Stating the facts is not a story. A story is about experiences, how you felt about them, and how they changed you or others.

Exposition (author commentary) is more important in memoir than in fiction. There is more telling than showing, but you can show a lot through colorful, detailed descriptions, action, and brilliantly applied dialogue.

**Develop the Stories:** These five techniques, which are explained in detail in my book, *Capture Life—Write a Memoir*, will have you writing like a pro:

**Break It Down:** Write subject by subject, event by event, emotion by emotion, person by person or whatever. Narrowing the scope of writing to incremental units prevents becoming overwhelmed. Later they can be sequenced in a logical fashion and transitioned.

**Apply Layers:** Write about a fact or event and then develop details around it. Explore the emotions and behaviors these incidents evoked. Reveal settings, feelings, reasons, and consequences. Add layer after layer of detail. (See run-throughs in the Appendix)

**Mine the Tidbits:** Capturing a life story is not about things of biblical proportions. You are not contemplating the world situation or the nature of the universe. Grow minor incidents into big stories. Memoir is about the quirky, the meaningful, the connections, the trivial made important. You could write a chapter about a toy, a wood stove, swimming in a pond, or a colorful hometown character. (Read David Sedaris. He is an expert at this.)

**Discover Defining Moments:** Search for things in your past that you (or whomever you are writing about) don't do anymore or that you suddenly started doing. Explore why. Behind these shifts in behavior are life events that provoked defining moments that changed everything. Examining them exposes temptations, brave confrontations, rallies from trauma, and humbling failures. These are powerful biographical jewels replete with lessons learned and evidence of growth. Describe the scars and festering wounds they produced. Human frailty and the struggle to overcome adversity draw readers in. On the other end of the spectrum, celebrate blessings and emotional bliss.

**Expose Rebel Jewels:** Look for instances when you or others were mavericks who broke away from the norm and did the unconventional. Rebel acts reveal brazen, risk-taking behavior resulting in devastating failures, blazing triumphs, or heartwarming experiences. Readers love such stories. One of my family's favorite stories is about two brothers who moved from Iowa to Oklahoma after the land run. One of them returned to Iowa and said, "I'd rather die trying to farm in Iowa than live trying to farm in Oklahoma." No doubt, a fascinating story resides behind that statement.

**The First Draft:** Give yourself permission to write a really shitty first draft and start writing. Don't stop. Write only for yourself. You are the audience. Consider this step as taking communion with yourself. This most likely will take several months. You have an entire lifetime to cover. Free flow. Write whatever comes into your head. Don't edit. The page count may be high, but not all of it will end up in the book.

Information doesn't have to be chronological. Think of settings, defining moments, embarrassing moments, sweet ones, fun ones, and hard ones. Write about what made you laugh, what made you cry, what made you wonder. Write about people, settings, feelings, crises, weather, travel. Write about a farm, a room, a neighborhood. Write about whatever.

Consider what was ordinary in your childhood that your descendants will never experience. Write about those things. They are treasures on the verge of extinction. Save them. Here are exercises designed to get you started:

(1) Write for fifteen minutes without stopping about your childhood room. Details will pop into your mind that suggest other things to write about.

(2) Pick a person and describe them in detail: clothes, hair, weight, smell, gait, features, temperament, laugh, hands, and eyes. Yes, write about eyes—the windows to the soul. Then write about the person's work, relationships, habits, preferences, personality, what they wanted, and whether or not they got it.

(3) Write about a traumatic event, a disappointment, something that threw you off your axis, or a defining moment that changed everything. Write about when you felt abused or unappreciated. Vent.

(4) Write about your roles: I was the kid who. . ., I was the woman who. . . , I was the girlfriend who. . . , etc.

Your first draft will most likely take on the tone of self-indulgence. It will be littered with *I's, me's* and *my's*. That's okay. Brag brazenly about accomplishments and your sparkling personality and charm. Whine and grouse about misfortunes. You, and only you, are the audience.

Keep the first draft, but copy it into a second file. This file will become the book's manuscript.

**The Second Draft—the Manuscript:** The audience is no longer you. It is readers. Think about their perspectives as you write. Take out anything you don't want in the final version. Rewrite the rest. Use the five techniques described above to develop what is left into robust stories.

Write incrementally by creating short stories. Give each one a beginning, middle, and end. Some stories will evolve into chapters. Others may be told in a few paragraphs. In a later draft, when you have a collection of stories, you will link them together in a logical sequence.

Layer on captivating, descriptive details. Add feelings. Take tidbits from the first draft and build them up. For example, here is what an elderly woman wrote:

**First draft:** Now in my seventies, every morning when I awake, I'm grateful for another day of independence.

**Second draft:** Every morning when I wake up and before my feet hit the floor, gratefulness washes over me. If I felt poorly when I went to bed, I'm surprised to still be here. I step onto a fluffy rug that is there because I'm into feel-good things these days. High heels and tight jeans are no more. In stores, I feel fabrics to make sure they pass the stroke test before taking an item off the rack. My pajamas are soft, the bedding high-thread-count Egyptian cotton, and the towels fluffy. The sofa is upholstered in fabric that feels like flannel and is topped with a throw that looks like angel hair and feels like bunny hair. A pillow filled with sumptuous feathers rests next to a fancy lace one that reminds me of Mom.

As you shape this second draft, avoid making your amazing qualities and accomplishments the main focus. Motivation—the driving force behind why and how you did what you did—is infinitely more intriguing than what you accomplished. And feelings—the burning consequences of those motives and actions—are more compelling than facts.

**Subsequent Drafts:** You will have many drafts. Each one adds another layer of richness to the story. (See run-throughs in the Appendix) After each run-through, you will look back and be wowed by how much better the writing is. That feeling is addictive. You learn that one more time will make a significant difference, and you don't want to stop.

With each pass, you build the manuscript up while editing it down by eliminating nonessentials. Delete with abandon. Find ways to write with as few *I's*, *me's*, and *my's* as possible. A good polishing will require many iterations of the book. Each one will enrich the story. Each one will be an accomplishment. Each one will make you grateful you went over the draft one more time. The goal here is not to bust out a book. It is to endure through revision, the slow and steady process of creating your own unique gem of a book.

Don't be intimidated by the prospect of multiple drafts. Creating them is good work. Revision is the process of writing. Enjoy that process. Drafts are where you make the story shine. Polish it as though you were creating a treasured work of art—because you are. You are articulating the essence of a human being.

**The First Page:** What influences readers, agents, and publishers the most is the first page. It is what gets a book published and sold. Consider beginning the memoir where the action is. Make the first sentence wildly intriguing so it grabs the reader. It is not unusual for a good writer to spend days on the first sentence and then revise it many times later. (See examples of first sentences in the Appendix.)

In the first couple of paragraphs, introduce the character and convey something intriguing about her world. Convey conflict, generate mystery, reveal challenges, and hint at the book's primary message. Your goal in the first page of a memoir (and the first page of every chapter) is to captivate the reader by creating intrigue. Make them want to know more. The reader needs a sense of time and place, so touch on setting. Avoid exposition, backstory, info dumps, and weather reports (unless central to the story). The first page has plenty of work to do without these intrusions.

Brent van Staalduinen recommends starting stories at a point when it's too late for the characters to turn back: someone got drafted, got pregnant, got a DUI, wrecked a relationship, hit a pedestrian, married the wrong person, got a psycho roommate, won in Vegas, lost in Vegas, saved a drowning child, adopted a baby, moved to Costa Rica, arrived in Africa, got so drunk he changed the wrong flat tire, or got so high he sat at a stop sign waiting for it to turn green.

**The Hook:** A thematic hook is important to the first paragraph, or at least to the first few pages, and it is carried throughout the book. It might even show up in the title or sub-title. A hook sums up the book's message in a clever way. It reels the reader in and makes him want to read more. Other minor hooks can be incorporated into chapters. Don't overdo.

**Thou Shalt Not Be Boring:** Poet Dylan Thomas said, "Someone is boring me. I think it's me." Triteness is probably the most common flaw in memoirs written by inexperienced writers. They just state the facts and fail to make characters and settings come alive. The sense of what appeals to readers is lacking. Avoid stating the obvious. Elevate the writing to entertainment. At some point, review every part of the book and take the writing to a higher level. Go through every sentence and search for a way to make it more expressive.

**Go Beyond Telling—Show:** You might characterize crotchety old Uncle Hank by saying he is grumpy or colorful. That is stating something. It is telling. By sharing stories about him that demonstrate his temperamental disposition, you are showing. Through his dialogue, actions, and expressions, you show he is grumpy without saying it outright. Explore why he has such a negative disposition. Add humor to your depiction of him, and he might love what you write. Crotchety people are often proud of their temperament.

**Portraying Real Characters:** In fiction, characters are made up. In memoir, the writer is dealing with real people, which requires discernment. As in fiction, you want to deliver characters who are sympathetic, even when dark sides are exposed. Your challenge as a writer is to manage that.

In memoir, a brother could be accurately described as a mean child, but a deeper description based on his motives might reveal he was intentionally playful and unintentionally a bully. Be kind. After all, he was a child. Sometimes child dictators grow up to be wonderful people. (Not always, though.) Take accountability for your role in sibling dynamics. Did you taunt him? Here's a thought: What did you do when you both encountered a common foe? And how is your relationship today?

Prospective character attributes are vast in number, giving a writer a plethora of qualities to write about. They include such things as: physical attributes, history, career, hopes, loves, fears, hates, needs, wants, regrets, flaws, frustrations, disappointments, grievances, habits, speech idiosyncrasies, achievements, obsessions, hobbies, losses, beliefs, skills, ethnicity, mannerisms, family dynamics, cultural influences, and coping mechanisms. If you worry about what to write about a person, this list should solve that problem.

**Write Strong:** Make every sentence meaningful. Take out all unnecessary words. (See *Sweeps - Find and Fix* in the Appendix.) Be ruthless about killing your darlings. Use adjectives sparingly and adverbs rarely (verbs are generally stronger by themselves). Write in active voice rather than passive when possible.

**Transitions and Flow:** Read the text out loud. You will discover awkward phrases as distracting as mismatched earrings. Rewrite them. Develop solid transitions from one sentence to another, one paragraph to another, and one chapter to another. Flow is vital to readability. It is what makes a story a page-turner. Begin and end paragraphs with the strongest sentences. Avoid long paragraphs where possible. Keep compound sentences to a minimum.

**WHAT SETS A MEMOIR APART?** If you want your memoir to stand out, consider these attributes:

- Good character development
- Brilliant setting descriptions
- Masterful use of inciting incidents
- Tension, conflict, curiosity, action
- Connections with historical events and culture
- Yourself as the author presented as a character

Make the reader feel. If you made him laugh, good for you. If you made him cry, you nailed it.

**INTERVIEW TECHNIQUES:** When it comes to interviewing older people, don't delay. Seize the moment. Every time someone dies, a wealth of generational stories are lost. Capture as many as possible. If you don't, they will soon be gone forever. Here are interviewing techniques:

- Don't tower over the interviewee. Lean in or sit on the floor at their feet.
- Dig deep for stories about themselves and you.
- Seek stories about parents, grandparents, etc.
- Probe for details, facts, and feelings.
- Explore historical events.
- Ask about how they found their partner and about love.
- Ask about their darkest moments and greatest fears.
- Seek out tragedies, failures, and regrets.
- Ask about successes.
- Ask what gave them joy.
- Ask what they would do differently if they could.
- Ask what advice they would give to the young.
- Ask about the most extraordinary moments, those they would like to live over again. Pursue details.

**Note:** Schedule a second interview after the interviewee has had time to think about these questions. You'll be amazed at what you get. The person may even have a list. Telling their story is a generous act. Thank them profusely. Acknowledge them in the book and send them a copy.

**PROBLEM CHARACTERS:** Understandably, people with secrets or uncomfortable pasts are going to worry about what you are writing. They have a lot at stake when someone they know is writing a memoir.

**Objectors:** If someone vital to the memoir insists they don't want you writing about them, respect that. There could be a legal issue if you write about them without permission. Before you give up, though, try this: Show empathy in your portrayal and introduce delightful, amusing interpretations. Describe Aunt Ethel as feisty, quirky, and zany instead of grumpy. Most likely, she is proud of her disposition and will enjoy your humorous portrayal of it. Let her read the draft, and invite her to contribute. (This may reveal fascinating reasons for her disposition.) Odds are, she will change her mind. She may become your greatest champion. If not, take her out (out of the memoir, not like, you know, out). Brace for the consequences. Later, when there is buzz about the book, these objectors often complain about being left out.

**Critics:** There will always be someone who won't like something you wrote. Don't let naysayers slow your roll. Write as though you are talking to someone who supports and champions you. Then, at some point, read the manuscript while in the head of your harshest critic and make adjustments to neutralize his or her objections when possible.

Experienced authors brush off bad reviews and harsh critics and concentrate on positive feedback. After you've spent years writing a book, there has to be a lot of good in it. Even when criticism is valid, it does not mean failure. The author created something. Who does that? In most cases, not the critics. Revel in the fact your creation exists.

**PRODUCING A MEMOIR:** Writing a memoir is one thing, producing it is quite another.

**Editing Memoir:** Toward the end of the memoir process, you face the prospect of editing and proofreading. Even pros struggle with this. How do you get all those nasty errors out of the writing? You probably won't, but try. (*Chapter 10 - Editing.*) Print and read from hard copy. Then read again out loud. Errors will pop out. Read again. Read until you find no errors (I've never been able to get there). When you think it's perfect, read again. You will find more. Then have someone else proofread. They will find errors. Read it again when they are through. You will find errors. At this point, you will understand why proofing is a curse to every writer.

Enough said. Don't argue. Don't object. Just do all that. You will regret it if you don't. I promise.

**Printing:** If you struggle with the printing process, join a writers' group and network. Engage a young relative to help. Imagine this: At an elderly person's birthday, anniversary, or Christmas party, every attendee receives a memoir authored by you and produced by some young whippersnapper. Such a multi-generational collaboration is the gift of legacy in its finest form.

**COPING:** Writing memoir requires a life review. This emotional process is draining. Writers experience ups and downs. One day the work is masterful, the next it's crap. Confidence in writing skill wavers. These feelings are common to all writers. The solution is to take breaks and let the book marinate. When you come back to it, you will see the beauty in it and push on through.

**Traumas:** Brace yourself for experiences that hit hard, such as discovering an error in an already published book or learning something you said hurt someone in a way you could not have imagined. You'll feel bad when such things happen, but consider this: The universe gives us the gift of days. Every day we get to start over. When you feel awful, wallow in it if you must, but consider the next day a new start. Bad is never forever. Say to yourself, "This, too, shall pass." Don't let mistakes take away your joy. You wrote a memoir. Whoo hoo! Bravo! You are the bomb.

Let's explore something else about writing that can give you joy—entering writing contests. In fact, you could enter your memoir in one. Contests are a challenge and it might take you awhile to get your land legs, but once you do, you are in for a ride. And once you win, you will chase that high.

*Chapter 13*

# Contest Strategy

*I usually know within the first couple of paragraphs if I have a winner.*—A contest judge

Contests contributed to my finding joy in writing. Winning the *Crème de la Crème Award* at a conference was like heroin. It was my first contest, which made the win especially sweet. I chase that high, knowing the experience is unlikely to happen again. Still, it feels good to try. So I try.

That incident produced a defining moment. Until then it was as if I were pretending to be a writer, even though I had written two books. When people asked what I did, I said, "I'm retired." Driving home after the win at that conference, for the first time, I said out loud, "I *am* a writer."

Since then, I've won or placed in many contests in poetry, essay, short story, and book categories. This includes four national/international book awards and Rose State's Outstanding Writer Award. Now I judge contests. I don't tell you this to impress, but to illustrate the opportunities contests offer and, hopefully, to convince you I know something about winning them.

**KEYS TO WINNING:** The keys to success in contests are authorship, determination, and strategy.

> **Authorship** requires continuous learning of the craft of writing, the art, and the business of the profession so the writer is an expert who delivers a polished entry.

> **Determination** means never giving up, being open to criticism, rebounding from losses, and submitting entries you believe in over and over.

> **Strategy** involves a smart approach to contests. It is true the writing needs to be top-notch, but don't underestimate the value of a strategic approach to entries. Playing the odds makes a difference. Many a fine writer lost out because of a lack of contest savvy.

An important component of the strategy that made my contest wins possible was establishing a season to write and a place to write. These support abundant creativity.

**A Season to Write:** Here is how my contest season works. I've done this every year for five years with good results—three to four Oklahoma Writers Federation, Inc., (OWFI) wins each year.

> **November:** I go to the *Eureka Spring Writers' Colony* to birth short stories, poetry, and essays for OWFI's annual contest.

> **December:** I polish the entries (revise/edit each ten times) and have at least one other person edit them.

> **January:** I submit the entries to the Oklahoma Writers' Federation, Inc.'s contest. I'm then postured to submit them to other contests throughout the year and to contests at writers' conferences. They can also be submitted for publication. Some entries end up in my books.

I take chapters from in-process books, turn them into stories that fit contest category requirements, and enter them. When these chapters are trimmed to meet contest word-count limits, they are so much better that I almost always replace the chapters in manuscripts with the entry version. I also take advantage of feedback from judges to enhance the writing.

**A Place to Write:** I go to the *Eureka Springs Writers' Colony* for the contest writing month of November. Hours are spent at a writing table overlooking a wooded area. Rates are economical and distractions minimal—no television, radio, phone, or friends and relatives. On weeknights, a family-style dinner is served with other writers. Locals hold potluck dinners, and writers read for them. The Colony also holds workshops. Check out Eureka Springs Writers' Colony at *writerscolony.org*.

**A Place to Win:** I attend several writers' conferences every year. Most have contests, and the odds of winning at these are better than at national contests.

**The Competition:** Writers often assume something is wrong with the judging when their exceptional, brilliant piece did not win something. Remember, it's a competition. A wealth of accomplished writers enter these contests.

As a judge, I've observed that contest entries usually present a normal curve. About twenty percent of entries fall at the top and at the bottom with the other sixty percent spread throughout the middle. Most contests have First, Second, and Third places with several Honorable Mentions or Finalists. You must break into the top ten to have a crack at winning or placing.

What is likely to disqualify your entry from the top ten or perhaps even plunge it to the bottom of the stack?

- Not meeting entry requirements
- Formatting improperly
- Going over the word count limit
- Entry doesn't fit the category
- Swear words (depending on the judge)
- Extreme political, cultural, religious perspectives
- Offensive topics
- The fatal blandness of academia (thesis-esque)
- Literary showing off: big words or flourish, such as: *we took our departure* instead of *we went home*.

**A COMPETITIVE ENTRY:** To be competitive, the craft absolutely has to be in there. Use the *run-through* and *sweeps* processes explained in *Chapter 8* and illustrated in the Appendix and the editing approach in *Chapter 10*. I believe these processes have contributed to my contest successes. They add a level of polish that gets me into top slots of the normal curve.

Editing is key. Proofread entries over and over. Ten times is not too many. This is why I take the whole month of December to polish and edit. Next, have a fresh pair of eyes review it. If you don't have someone else edit, you might as well not enter. I am always shocked at what my editors find when I think a piece is perfect. In my last entry, it was the simple mistake of using *lead* instead of *led*. How could I miss that having proofed the entry ten times and knowing better?

Every judge is different, but following is a list of entry shortcomings that cause most judges to conclude a writer is not competitive. Some flaws scream AMATEUR:

- Lack of voice/style: nothing distinctive about the writing
- Flat characters
- No setting descriptions or poor ones
- Overuse of clichés and similes or using poor ones
- Compound sentences with phrases punctuated improperly
- Data dumping—too much description/exposition at once

- Too much telling rather than showing
- Too much passive rather than active voice
- Unnecessary words (professionals write economically)
- Not applying point of view techniques
- Improper or inconsistent application of tense
- Improper or inconsistent application of person
- Improper subject verb agreement
- Triteness: stating the obvious/what reader already knows
- Literary showing off: big words and flourish
- Incomplete sentences (when not done stylistically)
- Use of: very, really, pretty, basically, actually, literally
- Overuse of adverbs and adjectives
- Excess words: the, that, all, any, just, quite, a lot
- Overuse of opaque words: they, them, there, this, it, things, items (use more descriptive words where possible)
- Overuse of would, could, had (suggests tense issue)
- Periods and commas outside of quotation marks
- Two spaces at the end of sentences
- Page numbers on blank pages
- Too many semi-colons (they are out of favor)
- Not using the Oxford comma in a series
- Inappropriate use and overuse of exclamation points
- Use of underlining, bolding, or excessive italics

**HOW TO GET FIRST PLACE:** In a contest, any award is precious. Nothing beats First Place, though. That should always be the goal. It may only get you Honorable Mention, but you would not have gotten that if you had not aspired to First Place. Here's what it takes to win:

**Nail the Craft:** You may get Honorable Mention with a fabulous story and mediocre craft, but First Place is unlikely. It's a competition. Others will have mastered both story and craft. As a judge, I see many fabulous entries lose out to the competition because of craft or mechanics. It's heartbreaking to observe deficiencies take out an exceptional piece from a talented writer.

**What Judges Look For:** In fiction categories, judges look for the elements mentioned in *Chapters 5, 6,* and *7.* Winning writers will deliver on these requirements.

In nonfiction categories, judges look for many of the same things. Outstanding nonfiction writers know many fiction techniques play well in nonfiction. You must compete with these astute authors. Study fiction. Those techniques will set you apart, especially in memoir, which is story-like.

Most nonfiction self-help and educational writing involves the "how to" factor. An entry in this category generally requires writing in second person (you, your, yours) and giving advice without being preachy. This is an art and something judges look for. It's a good idea to study the genre before entering this category.

There are three basic types of essays, each with different requirements: opinion, literary, and personal. Know which one the contest is looking for. Historically, structure requirements were generally the same for each type. An essay starts with a premise, presents arguments to support that premise, and sums up with a conclusion. A modern approach is more artful and allows for considerable exploration. Annie Dillard said, "There is nothing you cannot do with an essay; no subject matter is forbidden, no structure is prescribed." Not every judge would agree with her. *(*Read Dinty W. Moore's *Crafting the Personal Essay.)* I tried Dillard's creative approach on an essay and didn't win anything. The judge criticized the structure.

An article requires the standard journalism approach: a pithy title that grabs attention, a clear, concise leading sentence, and information fading down to the least important at the end in case the article must be cut to fit the space.

Even blogs have basic requirements. The main one is: Don't be boring. I've judged blogs and most of them are boring.

A writer's best bet for winning in a sentimental/nostalgia category is to make the judge cry. I love it when my editor complains something I wrote made her cry. This did:

> The piece began with a comment on how I had my grandmother and mother's hands. I described experiences of holding Mom's hand throughout the years, including when she was old and frail, and I was determined not to let her fall. I interjected thoughts of my being frail someday and that experience coming full circle. I revealed my amazement when, at sixty-something, I looked down and saw Mom's bony hands with blue, swollen veins and craping skin coming out of my sleeves.
>
> I wrote about holding my daughter's hand when she was a grown woman and Mom was gone. It felt the same. I told of the time I examined my baby granddaughter's soft, tiny hands and wondered whether, when she is grown, will they look and feel like those of three generations of women before her. I closed the piece by wondering whether I would live long enough to find out.

The topic alone made this entry perfect for the sentimental category. Every time I proofed it I teared up. My editor cried. The piece won First Place in a contest.

**Elicit Emotion from the Reader:** As a judge, I see entries all the time that reveal no emotion, and they draw none out of me. They are bland. Make the judge feel, and he will remember your entry. Most of my First Place wins were entries that made me cry or laugh every time I edited them— all ten times. If I were to read them today, I would feel.

**Be Aware of Trends:** There are trends in the realm of writing. Some are controversial. Whether you embrace them or not is a personal choice. Not doing so may not be technically wrong, but many judges appreciate writers who are up on accepted industry trends such as using only one space after a sentence and avoiding overuse of semi-colons and commas. Recognizing this, I asked young folks at the Apple store, "How do you use commas these days?"

A puzzled look crossed the face of one young man who said, "No one uses commas anymore."

Another said, "Don't use commas stupid."

The next said, "Put a comma where you would pause when you speak."

And then, this: "Just use a happy face."

The young folks may be technological geniuses, but they were no good to me at all on the matter of punctuation.

**Deliver A Memorable Title:** You want judges to remember your entry when they are looking for finalists. Here are examples of potential title improvement:

- *Mom* could be: *I've Been Mom-ed*
- *On Aging* could be: *The Inconvenience of Being Old*
- *Today's News Problems* could be: *The Void of Cognizance in the News*
- *Eating Disorders* could be: *An Adversarial Relationship with Donuts*

**Use Words In Unusual Ways:** I've used *eccentric* to describe a pickup truck and *overachieving* to describe a bushy beard. Grandchildren were named *Thing I* and *Thing II*, and a mooning incident was described as a *near sex experience.*

**Make Writing Unique/Original:** You've got to stand out. Do a run-through and assess everything. Avoid triteness. Go beyond the ordinary and what readers already know. Give them information they don't expect and do it in a unique way. Say something memorable. Surprise them. Judges love surprises.

**HOW TO SELECT A CONTEST:** Entry fees and playing the odds are factors that influence winning. National contests draw a lot of entries and the fees are usually high. For example: *Writer's Digest* is a prestigious contest but it draws thousands of entries and costs over $100 to enter. If you've got the money, it might be worth a try, but you can enter a number of $20 contests with better odds of winning for what you'd spend on one expensive long shot.

Regional contests sponsored by writers groups and conferences offer better odds. Not all conference attendees enter the contests, making the odds even better. Entries are usually in the hundreds. Educational institutions and library contests also have good odds. I've won four times at a library contest that has around 150 entries.

Match contests to your writing style. For example, a writer whose genre is humor, or horror, or sci-fi, or Chicken Soup for the Soul is unlikely to produce a scholarly feast strong enough to impress a judge in an academic-based, literary contest.

The more categories a contest has, the more the entries are spread out among them. If possible, find out how many entries are historically entered in each category. Increase your odds by entering low-volume ones. For example, entering a book in the *nonfiction* or *memoir* categories is going to result in stiff competition. In a more specific category, such as *aging* or *rural life*, odds are better. I played the odds and won a young adult fiction category, which is not my thing, but it had only sixteen entries the previous year.

Enter as many categories as you can. Focus on categories that are your forte, but try others. I've been surprised to win in poetry several times although it is not my strong suit.

**Entry Strategy:** Match your entry to the category. For example, there are subtle differences between *inspirational, nostalgia,* and *memoir* as well as between *horror, supernatural, sci-fi,* and *fantasy.* An *article* and an *essay* are substantially different and both are different from a *story.* Make sure you read each category's description. Note the requirements. Meet them. They will be the basis for judging.

Before I entered my first essay category, I ordered Dinty W. Moore's book, *Crafting the Personal Essay,* studied the genre, and got honorable mention. I have no doubt I would not have been competitive without that effort.

Unless stated otherwise, it's generally okay to be under the category word-count limit. Judges appreciate writers who keep entries lean and mean.

**Contest Sources:** To find contests, simply search online for "writing contests" or check out writing magazines. Here are contests for self-published books that have been good to me:

National Indie Excellence Awards
International Book Excellence Awards
USA Best Book Awards
Independent Book Awards
IPPY Awards

Other sources of contests include:

**Winningwriters.com** lists fee-based and free contests. It also lists contests to avoid.

**Mastersreview.com** is an online source of contests and advice for writers.

**Writing.shawguides.com** is a good source for contest information.

*The Writer* magazine (my favorite writer magazine) is a source of contest and conference information.

*Writer's Digest* magazine and website offer contests. Most writers consider these contests prestigious, but entry volumes are high and competition fierce. Local and regional contests are more viable.

*Poets and Writers* is another popular writers' magazine that contains contest information.

**Local contests** can be found by searching online for "writing contests." Add your state or surrounding states to the search. Many local contests are offered in conjunction with writers' conferences or events.

**Writers' conferences** almost always include contests. Check whether you have to attend to win. The *piece de resistance* for some is that winners are recognized publicly at banquets.

**Writers' groups** all over the country sponsor contests, which are usually posted online.

**Local libraries** often sponsor contests. Entry volumes are low and odds of winning good. It's nice to be recognized in your community. Winners may be announced on the local news.

**Universities** and other educational institutions run contests, often to scout for material for anthologies and other projects.

**What to Watch Out For:** There are scams and poorly run contests, some designed to make a profit. Before entering a contest, check with *winningwriters.com* or *writerbeware.com*. Don't sign your rights away and understand any contractual limits a contest places on your ability to publish your entry.

**Award Mills:** Opportunists run contests to identify naive writers to market their services to. Contestants are told their work is wonderful, but it needs polish (editing, rewrite, etc.) in order to appeal to the masses and to be a best seller. Then they try to sell the writer their services. They offer to obtain reviews and get the book in newsletters or magazines or on some list. Services are overpriced, quality is suspect, and none of this is likely to generate substantial sales. Such contests don't mean much in the industry. If you choose to enter one (I have done so), you may win something, but it is best to take the winning sticker and certificate and move on. And brace yourself for endless solicitation.

**Rights:** Universities and other organizations seeking works to include in anthologies or other publications may restrict rights for a few months after the entry is published. Then the rights revert back to the writer. In most cases, this is a good thing. The writer is published.

**JUDGES' PERSPECTIVES:** Judges are diverse and their personal preferences influence decisions. Also, in all genres, there are controversies about issues of craft, style, and methods. Where possible, neutralize anything that might be controversial in your entry. When editing, consider the perspective of the worst, harshest critic you can imagine and enhance the piece to mitigate his objections.

If you believe in a piece, don't give up if it doesn't win. Consider the judge's feedback and keep polishing. A different judge may judge differently. If one is harsh with feedback, consider the validity of his comments. Britton Gildersleeve, a writing professor advised me: *If you believe harsh criticism from a judge is undeserved, don't give up. Enter the piece in other contests. You may win.* I've done so several times. Reprisal is sweet.

A judge criticized my entry because a kid kicked a dog. He did so because he had just extracted a baby chick from the dog's mouth and Rufus was taking off after another. The judge said, "Under no circumstances should you endorse dog abuse." To hell with the chicks, I guess. The piece won the next year with a different judge.

Judges' preferences do influence outcomes. This is unfortunate, but unavoidable. Some of those biases include:

**Cultural and religious beliefs.** There are times when "golly" or "crap" won't do the job, but a judge may throw a piece out for a swear word. Whether you use such words or not is a personal choice. I normally use them when appropriate to the story and let the chips fall where they may (my apologies for the cliché).

**Scoring methods.** These vary among judges. A low score to one judge may be 30 out of 100 and another 60.

**Craft preferences and tolerance vary by judge.** Some will overlook errors while others throw entries out for minor transgressions.

**Format enforcement is subject to preferences.** This includes such things as margin requirements, page number placement, or indentation. Some judges are rigid and throw entries out for non-conformances while others overlook them, especially if the piece is strong. A minor error could cost you First Place, though.

**Category interpretations and requirements vary.** Judges view categories differently. In humor, one may say: "Make me laugh throughout." Another may say: "Just give me a clever ending."

**Literary preferences.** Professors will usually be more "literary" and have higher standards. However, they often give the best, most comprehensive feedback.

**Insensitive Judges.** Although judges are mostly thoughtful and helpful, some are not. Here are insensitive, unhelpful comments I've received:

"Dress a pig in a silk dress and it's still bacon."

"I don't know what the purpose of this story is except to depress us." (A boy's dog died.)

"This piece is akin to furnishing a living room by consulting a still of *The Brady Bunch*."

"Your characters are people others would want to avoid." (One of those characters was me.) Now, to be fair to the judge, I could have developed more sympathetic characters, but he could have made his point in a more constructive manner.

"If I could give you a zero, I would." This was on a book that won three other national book awards.

I received jarring feedback on an entry in a humor category:

- Wordy. Humor didn't work
- Comedic?—not so much
- Organization not clear
- Didn't tickle my funny bone
- Should be tighter/shorter

The judge gave me only 37 points out of 100. In another contest the same piece won First Place. It was read at the event. The audience laughed. I gloated. If I had given up after negative comments, I wouldn't have won the contests I've won. And I would not be writing this book. Always rally from disappointments. You'll find yourself eventually winning. Once you do, you will want to repeat that experience.

# SECTION IV

Printing/Publishing/Marketing

*The odds of you selling lots of books, making lots of money, and becoming famous are against you. However, if you are a writer with a fire in your belly, get your moxie on, become a raging, bad-ass marketeer, and drive through the smoke. Only those with the guts to do that are propelled to the top. People don't accomplish that to which they do not aspire. Just make certain you discover other reasons to write.*

*A writer is joyful when he knows it's not about the money. It's not about the notoriety. It's about the creation and, most importantly, the sharing of what he creates.*

*Chapter 14*

# Printing

*An author never finishes a book. He just abandons it and sends it to print.*

After years of working on a book, you'll wonder if it will ever be finished. It's difficult to know when to pull the plug and go to print. Polishing is a never-ending process. At some point, though, the author must cease writing and print. This requires he have a relationship with a printer, which is similar to an association with a babysitter who says, "Hey, kids, let's make a giant, talking, raisin-oatmeal cookie with bacon frosting."

To be a savvy book producer, you must nail the printing. This is a challenge because book production is a minefield for an apprentice. It thrusts him into a precarious dance with print/publishing vendors. In spite of the hype, few of them have the best interest of customers at heart. Since print on demand (POD) and self-publishing have flourished in recent years, printers and publishers are blended together so tightly it is impossible to disconnect the two. But I shall try.

If a book is to be distributed to family, friends, and other direct contacts, simply print it and share it. You can ask them to chip in on the cost, but if you plan to sell it on the open market, you are entering the world of publishing. This is discussed in the next chapter. For now, let's focus on printing.

Printing represents a substantial portion of the cost of a book. Prices fluctuate significantly between vendors. My books cost around $5 to print (includes shipping) at Amazon's KDP printing and fulfillment company.

Some writers go directly to electronic books (Amazon's Kindle, Barnes and Noble's Nook, and many more) without ever printing one. E-books are usually sold for less money since there are no printing, inventory, and shipping costs.

**THE MECHANICS OF PRINTING:** Printing, incorporating photos, designing a cover, and a number of other technical details related to producing a book are highly dependent on technology. Experts can be hired who you know are thinking, "I'm from tech support, and I'm here to make you feel stupid." And they are pricey. Even with their help, a writer cannot avoid technical functions. So befuddled writers are forced into the digital world through adult learning courses at libraries, colleges, book conferences, and seminars while asking, "Who signed me up for this?"

**Formatting:** Mechanics include the tedious process of formatting. When it comes to formatting, I ask myself, "My life has come to this?" It's not a fanciful task. I take no pride in it, and I know I won't find my happy there. But it must be mastered, and rather than lounge around in self-pity, I tell myself it's better than diabetes.

The format for submissions of manuscripts is different from the format for printing books. So a writer starts with the *manuscript format* and then he or a publishing company converts it to a *book format* when it's time to print. As a self-publisher, who can do whatever the hell I want, I skip the manuscript formatting that publishers require and go right for the book printing format when I write. (My editors are okay with that. Not all would be.)

> **Manuscript Format:** Writers who are seeking agents and publishers must follow standard manuscript formatting rules for submissions, which include 8 1/2" x 11," double spaced, left justified (ragged right margin), one-sided, one inch margins all around. (Search online for *Formatting: Modern Language Association - Standard Format.*) Most editors/proofers require standard format as well, and contests often follow standard format requirements.

> **Book Format:** As a self-publisher, I skip the manuscript format and write books in book format. This means I write in the book size 6 x 9, single spaced, right and left justified, two-sided, one inch margins all around. This eliminates reformatting later for printing. It also allows me to always know the book's size and how it will look to readers as I'm creating it.

I harp on the value of seasoned writers as advisors because they are an invaluable source of information for newbies. They know short-cuts and tricks to smooth out processes. Here is a taste of what they offer in the way of printing:

> Right and left justification creates gaps or crunched-up letters. These can be resolved by rewriting or by adjusting space between characters. Such space adjustments are also good for eliminating widows (a single word on a line at the end of a paragraph).

> Be careful about using exotic fonts. They distract readers and violate formatting standards. If you self-publish, you have more freedom to be expressive with fonts. However, readers tend to favor familiar ones.

> Consider the space impact of fonts when selecting one. Times New Roman provides for more characters per page

than most other popular fonts. EB Garamond provides a bit more space between lines for an easy read.

Note that italics don't show up well on some fonts. This can be a problem, especially in how-to books that tend to use italics.

A writer can learn such details through experience—sometimes painfully—or they can tap into the knowledge of the experienced.

The days of turning over a messy manuscript to a publisher and expecting someone to polish it up are over. Today's writers must deliver a polished product. Whether entering contests, sending out submissions, or self-publishing, a writer must dig in and deal with the mechanics in order to produce a quality piece. That is part of *authorship*.

**GALLEY COPIES (PROOFS):** Most writers will print copies in "manuscript form" periodically throughout the writing process for their own review and for editors. This is usually done at an office supply store or a place like FedEx. This will run around $30 per copy.

The first printing in bound book form is for galley copies, a fancy name for proofs (sample copies). This is done by a book printing vendor once the cover is designed and the text is edited and organized. I get mine from KDP Amazon.

Digital printing technology can deliver soft-back proofs bound in book form in about a week for around $5 each. If a writer is smart, he'll use such proofs to personally check every inch of the book and to give copies to beta readers and reviewers for their input. This is the final polish. Once the proofing phase is finished, the book is ready to print.

**INDUSTRY TRENDS IN PRINTING/PUBLISHING:** Printing and publishing industries are in unprecedented flux. The Internet, digital print on demand, electronic distribution channels, and innovative marketing models are revolutionizing the industry. Influence has shifted from publishers and agents to aspiring writers who can now self-publish. They are doing so in droves, and many are being taken advantage of. A plethora of companies have popped up to support self-publishing writers, which is a good thing and a bad thing. The business of printing has become a quagmire. A writer will encounter scammers and opportunists when they seek a printer. Learn about them in the next chapter.

**Print on Demand (POD):** With digital printing capability, a book is printed when someone orders it. This eliminates inventory management. Digital printing can quickly produce a single book at a viable cost, so it is possible to seamlessly sell, print, and distribute books in a couple of days through a print vendor. Many seasoned self-publishing writers use Amazon's KDP (Kindle Direct Publishing) for this, as do I. This company provides helpful online information and resources for writers.

Don't be confused by the label POD, which some publishing companies use to impress writers. Print on Demand is a printing process. It is not a publisher business structure. When vanity/subsidy publishers make a big deal out of being a POD company, know that today, almost every company uses this printing process. Even books by writing experts sometimes list POD as a publishing alternative. It is not. It is a printing alternative. Publishing alternatives are discussed in the next chapter.

**CAUTIONS:** With print companies tied up with publishing companies, the scene is set for taking advantage of inexperienced writers. It's a jungle out there. Here are situations to watch out for when seeking a printer:

Don't use anyone who solicits your business. Use printers recommended by experienced writers.

Don't give anyone money up front to print or publish without consulting an expert or seasoned writer.

Don't pay large dollars for printing. It should cost less than $5 to print most books.

Don't let anyone talk you into ordering a large inventory of books. Buy only enough copies for your immediate needs.

The more aggressive an organization is with selling services and package deals, the more determined you should be to avoid them. When a printer asks for more than $5 to print a book, insists on high-dollar up-front money, or requires large book orders, run.

**THE JOY OF A BOOK IN PRINT:** When I received the first shipment of my first book, I busted into the box, held a copy of *Out of Iowa—Into Oklahoma* in my hands and worshiped it. I hugged it, danced, and said out loud, "I am published." It was a defining moment. Many books later, I still get that rush when a first book order arrives.

Whether you go beyond the point of printing to publishing is a personal decision. If you don't intend to sell, the next two chapters will not apply to you, but you should read them. They include information that will help you avoid complications of the publishing industry that bleed over into printing. Knowledge is your friend.

---

Note: I refer to Amazon and Amazon KDP (Kindle Direct Publishing) numerous times in this book because those are the channels I use for printing, sales, and distribution. (Amazon has over 50% of the book sales market.) This strategy has worked well for me as well as for most self-published writers I know, and it's the model with which I am most familiar. It is a simple, workable approach. There are others. Each writer must find his own path.

*Chapter 15*

# Publishing

*No one interested in being published in our time can afford to be so naive as to believe a book will make it merely because it's good.*—Richard Curtis

The publishing arena is where a book is promoted and sold. Unless you plan to sell your book, there is no reason to publish. Print and you're done. If you cross the line into selling, you're entering the realm of publishing.

**PUBLISHING OPTIONS:** There are three basic tracks to publishing:

> **(1) Traditional publishers:** Major publishing houses and their specialty subsidiaries (called imprints), mid-sized publishers; and small publishers.
>
> **(2) Vanity and subsidy publishers**
>
> **(3) Self-publishing**

**Traditional Publishers:** The qualities that most distinguish traditional publishers from others are: (1) they do not ask writers for money up front, (2) the larger ones have the muscle to get books into large bookstores (only about 20% of book sales are made at these stores) as well as libraries and retail stores: Walmart, Target, airports, etc., (3) they require the writer have an agent, and (4) they finance the production of books and make money only when books sell. Consequently, they are highly motivated to sell.

Publishing through one of the major publishing houses or their imprints (subsidiaries) is viewed as the brass ring by many writers. Several medium-sized publishers are also prestigious. Although small traditional publishers don't have the clout of the larger ones, they are more nimble and are a good match for unestablished writers.

Major publishers and their imprints are blockbuster focused. The prospect of a new writer breaking into that part of the industry is slim. It's not unusual for writers who have made it into the big leagues to tell tales of multiple rejections over a period of many years. Kathryn Stockett's book, *The Help,* was "snatched up" after five years of required rewrites and over sixty submissions.

The writer's cut of revenues with these publishers is paltry. Royalties on net sales run only about 7.5%, and an agent takes 15% of that. (If you want to make your head hurt, go online and study royalties and agent fees.) A writer aspiring to the big leagues must be prepared to give up the rights to his book, to market like crazy, and to have a social media platform with substantial followers ready to buy his book.

The writer loses control of book production processes, such things as the title, cover, and pricing. He is likely to be subject to mandated re-writes. It is not unusual for a publisher to take eighteen months from the time of the contract to get the book out. In contrast, a self-published book can be on the market a week after the author finishes it and at little cost, often well under $1,000. A writer asked me what it cost to get a book on Amazon. I answered, "Nothing," which shocked her. But it is true. The biggest costs are typically the pre-publication expenses of editing (ranging from several hundred dollars to several thousand) and book cover design (around $250). In spite of the downsides of the traditional model, many writers chase that golden ring and aspire to publish their books through the majors.

**Vanity/Subsidy Publishers:** *Vanity* businesses require authors to front the money to produce their books. This includes the publisher's profit. *Subsidy* businesses share in providing up-front money, but they often recoup their investment before the author gets any of his. By getting money up front from the author, these companies are guaranteed a profit whether the book sells or not. So they are not as incentivized to sell as traditional publishers.

Most retail bookstores shun vanity/subsidy books. Because of industry prejudices, these companies are unlikely to label themselves as what they are. Writers must figure it out. A writer giving a publisher money up front to produce and sell a book distinguishes a vanity company. Experts generally advise serious writers to avoid them. A writer who had signed a contract with one said, "It was as though I was sitting in a friend's recliner pleading with him to make his Rottweiler stop licking me."

**Self-Publishers:** Introduction of the self-publishing model has shifted power from a publisher's playpen to a writer's wonderland. This model—made possible by online bookstores, electronic books, digital printing, and print on demand—has revolutionized the industry. It gives writers control and generates the most income from each book sold.

Amazon pays 30% royalties on e-books and up to 70% on print books. Approximately 80% of books produced today are published outside the traditional publishing arena. They are a blend of vanity, subsidy, and self-publishing. It is impossible to determine how many fit into each category, but Amazon easily has over 50% of the entire book market.

Historically, commercialized publishers screened out substandard books unlikely to generate substantial revenue. With writers self-publishing, that process doesn't happen. Quality checkpoints no longer exist. Books with little chance of commercial success are flooding the market. The onus for producing a high-quality book is on the self-published writer—another reason to become an expert.

The growth of companies seeking a piece of the self-publishing pie has produced a sea of choices for authors. It has also presented problems. Complicated models and misleading labels imply to unsophisticated writers that if they sign with a company they are self-publishing when they are not. If you pay someone to publish and they buy the ISBN and are listed on Bowker and other book registers as the publisher of record, they are technically the publisher. For this reason, I formed a publishing company and register my books under its name. And I get my own ISBNs.

Self-publishing is essentially running a business and this requires knowledge, time, and effort. However, it is inexpensive and a sure way to get a book out quickly while maintaining control of the process. There are many other advantages that come with this model, but problems for writers have emerged. They are complicated and beyond the scope of this book. If you plan to go this route, study up. Hundreds of books on self-publishing can be found on Amazon. Some I've read are listed in the Appendix.

Both *smashwords.com* and Amazon's KDP provide significant writer education online, and *The Masters Review* is an online source of advice for new writers. A checklist of action steps for self-publishing is included in the Appendix of *Capture Life—Write a Memoir.* For a simple solution, self-publishing authors should consider this straightforward model:

(1) Use KDP Amazon to print books for the author's inventory for direct sales and to do fulfillment (print and ship) for sales on Amazon.

(2) Use Amazon to sell printed books and electronic books (Kindle). They record sales, take their cut, and send the author his share.

(3) Use your website. Link it to Amazon to sell books.

Because of user friendly technology and excellent customer service, an apprentice writer can avoid many problems with this model. It is the one I and many writers I know use. Other reputable publishing models exist. Serious marketing enthusiasts may supplement this Amazon model with contracts with other companies, such as Smashwords, to expand into other sales channels. Doing so complicates the publishing process and may not yield enough sales to make the extra effort worthwhile.

With so many publishing methods, vigilance is advised for unsophisticated writers wading into the publishing arena. Tapping into the knowledge of seasoned writers can be the bridge to a good publishing decision.

**PROSPECTS:** For most writers, engaging a literary agent and a major or mid-sized publishing house is a long shot. A small, traditional publishing company is more viable. They give good support, don't ask for money, and can make your book a reality. Research their financial viability. In this volatile market, some companies don't survive.

Under none of the publishing scenarios (traditional, vanity/ subsidy, self-publishing) is a writer likely to experience a substantial income stream. Glory stories about authors getting rich represent a minuscule portion of the writing population, although they are highly publicized. Stories of self-publishing on Amazon being a springboard to a major publishing company contract are also exaggerated. Simply stated, it is possible but unlikely your book will be a big seller. If you find this disheartening, consider this: Chase your dreams but be honest about why you write. Don't let industry bluster define dreams for you or determine the criteria for your success.

**SCAMMERS AND OPPORTUNISTS:** Scammers and opportunists chase authors who are looking to publish. Scammers make promises they don't keep. Opportunist keep their promises but play on writers' naiveté to take advantage. In both cases, money flows from the writer to them. If you access their websites or respond to their advertisements, brace yourself for a hard sell. Here is how they operate:

> They ask for your manuscript and then notify you it is remarkable (which is what they tell everyone). Next, they request a substantial amount of money to produce and sell the book. You send them $2,000 to $10,000. (You can self-publish a book for as little as $500.) They must sell a lot of books for you to recoup your investment, let alone make anything. Can they do that? It's unlikely. Do the math. When a writer complains his book is not selling, they ask for more money to fund more promotion. Many people give it to them. Don't be one of those people.

Run the numbers. Be skeptical of dubious sales projections and exploitative contract provisions. Remember this: Although it is true earnings are a function of promotion, the key to selling a book is not the promotion someone else does. It's what you do. Don't be a victim. Use due diligence to check out companies and use healthy skepticism when their sales pitches hype glorious results.

The best way to find a publisher is through writer friends. Here are points to consider when selecting a publisher:

Companies advertising for first-time writers to give them a break are actually seeking the naive to get them to part with their money.

Royalty percentages may be misrepresented and overstated because of complicated and vague formulas.

Logos of vanity/subsidy companies on your book can cause a negative connotation to be attributed to it.

Don't be taken in with glory stories of wealth, fame, and a top-selling book. Success stories are often distorted and represent a small percentage of writers. Consider the failure rate, which is somewhere around 95% to 99%, depending on how success is defined.

Be skeptical of paying to get a book on distributors' lists. Doing so does not mean bookstores, libraries, or retail stores will order it. They probably won't.

Don't pay for marketing/advertising unless a cost benefit analysis suggests it will generate enough net cash to you to make the investment worthwhile. In spite of the hype, the likelihood of that is remote.

Don't give anyone a list of your sales contacts without analyzing the situation. Keep them for yourself. You can sell direct to family and friends and realize a larger profit margin. Why give anyone else a cut?

Be skeptical of book doctors who advertise. They are often overpriced and the quality is suspect.

Never pay for a book review (it's unethical). Don't pay a reading fee to an agent. Work with agents who are members of the Association of Authors' Representatives.

How to avoid scammers and what to look out for in contracts are included in my book, *Capture Life—Write a Memoir.* The Alliance of Independent Authors's book *Choosing A Self-Publishing Service* is also a good source.

Protect Yourself: Read contracts carefully. Look out for exclusive arrangements and provisions related to rights. Research potential publishers. Use *writersbeware.com,* a site that reports complaints and scams and *TheCreativePenn.com/watchdog.* And, as I've said over and over in this book, seasoned writers know who the reputable businesses are.

**Legal Issues:** Legal landmines surround any form of writing. Copyright, privacy, and libel laws apply. Anyone can sue, whether they have a case or not. Problems are avoided, or at least mitigated, by being truthful, following referencing standards, and writing gently about people. Still, legal issues are worrisome. Every time I hear a lawyer speak about writing at a conference, I want to stop, drop, and roll. I consider not publishing again, or even not writing, which is like losing my breath.

Then I consider this: I was seventy-one years old when I first went 120 mph. I've survived men in suits, rednecks in four-wheel-drive diesel trucks, and disco. I'm more afraid of the Internet than I am of lawyers. So I regroup, get my freak on, put on my big girl stretch pants and decide to not let legal issues detour me from my purpose. If legal worries consume you, ask yourself: Do you want your story to remain untold because of lawyers? Err on the side of caution if you must, consult an expert if you feel the need, check facts when possible, but deliver.

**THE FROSTING:** Don't let downsides of publishing discourage you. Writers who persist succeed. Remember, you can guarantee success by defining it on your own terms.

*Chapter 16*

# Marketing

*The Audacity of Possibilities*

Once you decide to market a book, you enter the realm of running a business. You'll be dealing with record keeping, taxes, business structure, licenses, and other aspects of being in business. You'll have a file cabinet, bank account, credit card, and possibly an accountant and attorney. This is a far cry from literary meanderings. But if you are a writer focused on selling, get your moxie on, become a raging, bad-ass marketeer, and drive through the smoke. Only the people with the guts to do that are propelled to the top.

The first rule of selling has nothing to do with these things, though. It is about the product. Marketing and sales efforts will be for naught without an exceptional product, especially in the competitive business of selling books. Without that, nothing will bring success in the marketplace. You must compete for readers with thousands of ambitious, seasoned, skilled, and connected writers. If you are up for that, listen up.

**A SELLABLE BOOK:** Your book must be top-notch to sell. An agent who gets hundreds of manuscripts a week will read only the first paragraph or two of many of them. Is yours good enough to make her read on? Would someone picking up your book in an airport gift shop read past the first paragraph and be motivated to buy? For an example of a book that does that, read the prologue to *Water for Elephants*, by Sara Gruen. You can do so on Amazon by clicking on the *Look Inside* feature. No doubt, the prologue sold that book.

**THE SELLING PROCESS:** Selling is a function far removed from the creative process of writing. It's about supply and demand, competition, promotion, branding, pricing tactics, marketing strategy, financial analysis, and business principles. To share a creation broadly, you must deal with these, and you must promote the heck out of the book. To sell lots of books you need to tap into the masses.

Companies will offer to market your book for a fee, usually a hefty one. They really can't do that effectively, although their sales pitch will suggest they can. You, as the author, must sell it. Even if you have an agent and a publisher, you still must sell. When it comes to generating sales, you are *it*.

Whether you self-publish or chase agents and publishers, you are in for a challenge when you decide to sell. It's tough to do so successfully under any scenario. That is why so many companies try to get money up front from writers. This assures they make a profit regardless of sales volume.

**Pricing Strategy:** You can get advice on this by reading books on publishing and marketing. Make certain they are written by authors. Publishing companies put out such books to entice writers to sign with them. In general, it's best to avoid companies that solicit your business.

Many writers play with pricing regularly (called price pulsing) since online book-selling companies like Amazon allow price adjustments. (This is a reason to not set a price with Bowker when getting an ISBN so the price is not on the barcode.) I don't claim to understand the strategies for marketing on Amazon. No amount of study has gotten me there. Since I'm not primarily focused on selling and making money, I don't play with pricing. I keep it simple:

- Price all books at $12 online
- Price all books at $10 when selling direct
- Price all e-books at $2.99
- Don't change prices (pulse pricing)
- Sell exclusively through Amazon and Kindle
- Sell through my website, which is linked to Amazon

**Best Seller Lists:** The strategic timing of sales can get a book on Amazon's top seller list, but it's complicated. Most publishers know how to make this happen. Doing so is a short-lived accomplishment, and I don't know what it gets a writer other than bragging rights. Astute writers and people in the industry know best seller lists can be manipulated and a best seller brag may or may not mean much. Still, I give credit to any writer who can make this happen.

**What Won't Generate Sales:** Even with all the hype about having a platform, most writers don't realize substantial sales through social media. Book signings, press releases, reviews, and radio and television appearances won't generate much either. Taken altogether, these efforts can make a difference. Will they allow you to quit your day job? Probably not. Giving speeches is the most lucrative for me, but the most I've ever made was $330 gross. Net is half that amount because of printing and shipping costs. A writer realizes even fewer dollars per book through other sales channels if an agent, publisher, and seller take a cut.

Selling to other writers cannot be counted on for much revenue. Like the general public, authors have a plethora of reading options to choose from, and they tend to read only in their genre.

Another challenge to selling is that not everyone is a reader. Most likely, about half of your relatives and friends don't read books. This is disheartening, but it's reality. Few writers sell "lots of books." Breakthrough authors are loudly touted, but they are a minuscule portion of the hundreds of thousands of authors producing each year. This is why the premise of this book, that you define success according to aspects of writing that bring you joy, is important. You don't have to give up your dream of fame and fortune, but focus on other writing activities that enrich your world.

**BRANDING YOURSELF:** Branding yourself as an author is vital to successful selling. Don't focus so much on a book title that your author name takes second place. If possible, use your author name on websites and other social media venues. Famous authors do this. Don't be bashful about hyping yourself.

**Image:** I'm writing about this subject because few experts do so. There are things you need to know about how you present yourself. This is important because:

> You can never make a neutral impression.
> It is either positive or negative.
>
> You can't undo a first impression.

Most writers, including myself, tend to dress like French cafe slouches. We are a comfort-seeking bunch and not much into the pretentiousness of being trendy and well dressed. Fashionistas don't write. If you are serious about presenting yourself as a professional writer, you would do well to take image seriously. Appealing to agents and publishers, impressing fans, and making your mark as a successful, serious writer is tough to do if you look like Columbo or Larry the Cable *Gal*.

Make a conscious effort to portray yourself in a light that is consistent with career goals. When pitching a book, it's important to look like someone an agent or publisher would be proud to represent and to present. They know how you look when they meet you is the best you are ever going to look. So step it up.

Layers of colorful garments make a writer look like a donkey cart. An iridescent garment distracts an agent with thoughts of a glow light. Facial piercings, snake tattoos, or goth netting hint at anti-social leanings, as do overachieving beards. A complicated-patterned garment makes a person look like wallpaper. Bright, multi-colored clothes might cause a writer to be mistaken for a piñata, in which case a publisher would imagine beating her with a stick instead of publishing her book.

If you choose to sabotage your career by showing up for a publisher interview dressed so sloppily you spark images of a homeless Nick Nolte, save yourself some time and take your big, bad self on down to Jake and Elwoods, elbow your independent, rebel psyche up to the bar, and have a couple of beers with Vinnie while your beard grows.

The writer's objective should be to appear smart, sharp, dependable, enthusiastic, and professional—like he is someone who has it together and can deliver. Appearance is an integral part of that overall impression. Once an initial image is portrayed, it is not easily undone.

Decision-makers must be able to visualize a writer in the role of selling his book. They also need to feel good about their decision because they must justify it to peers, superiors, financial decision-makers, and others in the industry. Don't embarrass them, and don't put them in the position of having to defend you because you decided image is not important. Make them proud. Give them what they need to sell you and your book.

**PROMOTION vs CREATION:** It's easy to get swept up in industry hype that defines success as volume of sales, but that is not for everyone. Consider opportunity costs—the money, time, and other activities that must be given up to market a book. If you take selling seriously, you'll be spending two intense years on functions that distract from family, work, recreation, and your next creation.

Those distractions are why I do a soft launch, which involves a month or two of intensity. Then I move on to just dabbling in sales while focusing on my next book. This decision is partly due to my age. Time is precious. But even younger people, especially those with family obligations, should strategically and rationally determine how to allocate their time. It would be prudent to factor realistic sales outcomes into such decisions.

You don't have to sell. You can consider yourself successful as an author when the book is produced. You did it. It exists. It is out there for generations to come. Whether the book sells a little or a lot, it is shared.

Give yourself the gift of brand. Take advantage of the edge it offers. Whatever branding and imaging choices you make, know this: You are a writer. You are somebody. Shine, writer, shine. And don't let anyone or anything throw a shadow on that sparkle.

# SECTION V

A Personal Path

*Passion is about something that makes you feel as though you are enough just by being. Nothing else is needed to define you. Sharing passion with others promotes a sense of purpose. And sharing is the path to mattering. Discover your passion in writing.*

> *"Once you recognize within yourself a hunger for something beyond just continuing, once you taste even the possibility of touching the meaning in your life, you can never be completely content with just going through the motions."—Oriah Mountain Dreamer from "The Invitation."*

*Chapter 17*

# Be Bold

*Wrap your writing in a pretty package, for there is
joy in achievement and bliss in finding passion.*

What if you wrote as if you knew you were dying? Imagine
the freedom this approach would foster. This complements the
central premise of this book, which is to write whatever the
hell you want and write it whatever way you want. This may
cause you to ask, "Doesn't all this talk of craft, rules,
requirements, image, and pleasing your audience restrict
writers and contradict this premise?" Let me clarify.

If you don't plan to share what you write, you are the
audience, and you have free rein. If you plan to share it,
you have an audience. That comes with responsibilities.
Readers have expectations, and they want entertainment
and information. It is your job as the writer to give it to
them. You signed up for that when you decided to be a
writer and to share what you write. It's a matter of respect
and integrity to deliver a quality product and to
demonstrate at least some degree of *authorship*. You see,
writing is giving. And it goes both ways. You give readers

what they want and need, and they honor you. Wrap your gift in a pretty package. Write well.

**THE ENTERTAINMENT FACTOR:** To entertain, you must first be interesting. When writers talk about voice, show vs tell, point of view, tense, person, setting, and all the other elements of writing, their objective is to use those techniques to entertain and inform. These tools are the path to giving the audience what they desire. When we as writers don't deliver, we disappoint. We fail to honor our promise.

I ordered a comedic book on Amazon. Plentiful errors intruded on the humor. As a reader, I was disappointed. I understood that the writer was not skilled, but another set of eyes would have eliminated the clutter and made the book more engaging. Still, it exists. The writer put himself out there and created something. You've got to give him credit for that. I can't help but wonder, though, what he could have accomplished with a good editor.

**FINDING JOY THROUGH ACHIEVEMENT:** When you choose your path to finding joy in writing, consider this: There is joy in achievement. If you take *write whatever you want* and *write it anyway you want* seriously, you might change "what you want" when you realize the benefits of being good—really good—at something. I never thought about being an expert at writing initially. I just saw myself as being creative. Now that I'm reaping the benefits of learning, I find pleasure where I never expected it. The feeling of accomplishment *authorship* offers builds pride. Achievement is a sublime ego booster, a confidence builder, and even a source of joy. It gives a writer the gift of a sense of purpose.

**BE AUDACIOUS:** To strike a balance between creative expression and complying with traditional publishing expectations, a writer must walk a line. He has more freedom of expression if he self-publishes. For example, in my first memoir, I wanted to share life's lessons with children, grandchildren, nieces and nephews, and future generations. I hoped to reach into the future—beyond my time on this earth—and share wisdom.

I imagined my grandchildren reading my life story someday when I'm no longer here and they are teens on the threshold of life. I hoped something I said in my book would make a difference in their lives. But all that advice could be too preachy and turn them off. So I adopted a non-traditional approach. I put a list of *lessons learned* in the Appendix. Since I was sixty-something at the time, the list was so long that I threw in playful words of wisdom here and there to keep the interest of young, frisky people who have distracting electronic devices and short attention spans. For example:

- Don't pack vibrating children's toys in luggage when flying.
- If the baby's hand is in the way during an ultra-sound, it's a boy.
- If you swear in front of children, don't follow up with "Oh shit!"
- If a man is quiet, it doesn't necessarily mean he's mysterious. He may just be stupid.
- Don't ask older people how they feel unless you really want to know.
- Stay away from people with guns who are looking for their anti-depressants.
- March Madness is not a sale at Macy's.

Because my writing style was to insert questions throughout the memoir, the Index consisted of questions with associated page numbers. Readers could pretty much find their way around the book by the questions asked:

- How many quarters are there in football game?
- If I lie down on the sidewalk, would you draw around me with that chalk you policemen carry around with you?
- You are kidding, right?
- Whose trombone is this in my car?
- Mom, you want a tattoo? How about this skull and crossbones? It's not poison. It's about pirates. We like pirates.
- You shouldn't walk your dog at night. If you don't come back, can I have your car?

It's unlikely a publisher would allow such breaks from tradition, but with self-publishing, I could express myself with abandon. In a more significant break from protocol, I made up ridiculous reviews—with full disclosure, of course:

A sensitive, thought-provoking, and often humorous exposé of the events and people that shaped a remarkable life . . .Wesley Huntington, II, Dyslexic Writers Foundation

. . . If I was a bettin' man, I'd bet the w-o-o-man writin' this has nice child-bearin' hips. . .Jim Bob (Catfish) Hunt, Oklahoma River Review

This book inspired me to get rid of Ralph, redecorate the house, and get my name off the grandkids' loans. I ain't co-signing no more for NOBODY. . .Ms. Effie May Watts

The author made me realize I was trying too hard, so I quit. . .Stella Steward, Retired Homemaker

---

Note from the Author: There were no reviews, so I made some up. This is an integrity gap. Sometimes I do things I shouldn't.

This fit of whimsy meshed with one of the sub-themes in the memoir wherein I made the point that Grandma GoGo is not always a good role model and has legitimately earned the title of Aunt Nik who swears. When I asked people what was their favorite part of the book (my favorite question for readers), they almost always mentioned one of these deviations from the norm. A writer friend, stunned by these unconventional antics, asked, "Is there any Karaoke in there?"

**Buck Up:** Don't follow a path because others defined it for you. Ralph Waldo Emerson said, "To be yourself in a world that is constantly trying to make you something else is the greatest accomplishment." One of my favorite author experiences illustrates this point:

> While preparing to speak to a conservative group, I worried whether to talk about my newest book, *Near Sex Experiences.* I had concerns about the audience accepting it. However, I was proud of the book and decided to be bold and include it. I put copies on a table with other books to be sold. The book sold out immediately after the meeting, and a lady called out to me, "Hey, Nikki, you are out of the sex book." I went to my trunk, restocked the table with "sex books," and sold every one.

**AN EMOTIONAL ROLLERCOASTER:** One day you conclude your in-process book is a brilliant, captivating piece of literature. The next day it's rubbish. You vacillate between pride and embarrassment. One day, you are the bomb and the next you conclude readers will view what you write as folly and your writer cohorts will decide you're an idiot.

Writers are too hard on themselves. Emotional distractions and insecurities interfere with progress. When the rollercoaster takes you to the bottom, take a break. Talk to someone who champions your efforts, (thank them in the Acknowledgments), peruse your list of learning activities and accomplishments, and look in a mirror and do a therapeutic Al Franken, "I am good enough."

The rollercoaster continues after the book is written. You get a bad review, find an error in an already published book, discover you violated a publishing requirement, or worse yet, realize something you wrote hurt someone in a way you didn't anticipate. Accept the ups and downs. Life is like that, and so goes your book. The solution is to start the next one. Resilience is the balm.

**COURAGE SQUARED:** A sense of purpose flourishes when people step out of their comfort zone. Doing so is a role-modeling opportunity. By showing how rewarding writing can be, you influence others. They may stand on your shoulders and write something themselves.

Everyone's interpretation of what they read is filtered through their internal belief system. For this reason, readers are judgmental, and there is always someone who doesn't like what you wrote. If you find yourself caught between pleasing readers or pleasing yourself, I vote for the latter.

Don't restrict yourself because of someone else's values. You are the author. Be bold. If you use this quote: "'Balls,' said the queen, 'if I had balls I'd be king,'" have the guts to spell out "balls." If "bummer" won't do the job, use a swear word. If someone doesn't like it, they don't have to read it. I got gutsy and chose a brown cover for this nonfiction book on writing, put a woman smoking a cigar on it, and used the word *hell* in the title. Who does that?

Don't let anyone's judgment rob you of the self-expression that brings you joy. Criticism is no reason to spiral into an existential crisis. Hey, you wrote something. That's killer. Toughen up. You're in the entertainment business. Right and proper is not entertaining.

Don't underestimate the therapeutic value to yourself and others of you being authentic and bold. Find your sweet spot, demonstrate courage squared, and express yourself fearlessly. Shape your world so it taps into your own special talent. Give the gift of writing only you can give. Be a joyful, purposeful, unapologetic scribe. Be that person.

# APPENDIX

# Index

# RUN-THROUGHS—LAYERING

The run-through process involves going over a working draft numerous times during the revision phase of writing, each time with a specific objective in mind. This is called *layering*. Every pass layers on another level of depth and shine. The composition becomes increasingly robust with each pass. Some run-throughs go quickly while others are tedious and require considerable time and detail work. Some may not be necessary for certain projects or for seasoned writers. If this layering process is intimidating, keep this in mind: Going over and over a manuscript and refining it is revision and revision *is* writing. (Note: If the following terms or rules are unfamiliar, Google them.)

---

- **Establish an overall theme:** Introduce it in the first chapter, thread it throughout the book (don't overdo), and zap it in the ending. Sub-themes can be incorporated throughout or limited to certain chapters. Tie them to the main theme, where possible, and resolve them in the ending if needed.

- **Create structure:** For fiction, outline the story or build a storyboard to create a narrative arc. For memoir and other nonfiction, rearrange memoir stories or other content into a logical sequence, usually after the first draft is completed. Use the table of contents to massage the order. Structure is fluid. Revise as needed. Ensure smooth transitions.

- **Organize the book and chapters:** Create a beginning, middle, and end for the book and for each chapter, and establish an overall narrative arc. Although this is a fiction concept, memoir and other nonfiction writing can benefit from a narrative arc.

- **Establish flow and manage the pace:** Build up low spots. Don't let the middle slump—up the stakes, increase the action, or introduce sub-plots. Surprise the reader, even shock him. Continuous emotion or action exhausts the reader, and he may feel as though he's been handcuffed to Kevin Hart. Spread out action. Insert exposition, dialogue, and narration after intense scenes to slow things down.

- **Create transitions:** Assure flow from sentence to sentence, paragraph to paragraph, and chapter to chapter. Leave each chapter with a teaser: an intriguing thought, a profound question, a high or a low point, or a precarious one. Delay resolution to the next chapter so readers read on.

- **Assure point of view (POV) consistency:** Establish the POV in the first few sentence of the book and in each scene/chapter. Avoid head-hopping from one POV to another within a chapter or scene unless doing so strategically. Clue the reader in on any changes. (This is a major problem area for many writers.)

- **Review point of view and name use:** In fiction, use the point of view character's name the first time you mention him or her. Then use third person (he or she) for the rest of the scene/ chapter. Don't overuse first and last names together after introducing a character's full name. Pick the first or last name to use throughout a scene or chapter.

- **Determine Tense:** Check for consistency of tense by sweeping for exceptions. Variations are appropriate—even necessary— but they should be intentional and not jolt or confuse readers. If you find yourself using *had* or *would* often (a common practice of new writers), reconsider the tense. Research tense on line. It's complicated.

- **Develop characters and construct character arcs:** Primary characters should be complex, flawed, and sympathetic, even the bad guys. Give them special abilities, unusual traits, a past and a future, and good and bad qualities. Disclose personalities and physical attributes. Reveal temperaments, grievances, vulnerabilities, strengths, relationships, hopes, regrets, and losses. Make every character, no matter how minor, interesting in some way—no cardboard characters. Main characters should evolve—change over time.

- **Use names to define characters:** Names do a lot of work by implying information about a character. Keep a list of unique, interesting names. Even minor characters can have revealing names—a mechanic named Ode, a woman named Roxie, a dog named Knuckles. And then there is Uncle Skillet, his brother Bucket, and Aunt Weezie.

- **Add dialogue and quotes:** Use these to describe characters and to move the story forward. Dialogue and the actions surrounding it are *show—don't tell* opportunities. Sprinkle them throughout.

- **Show—don't tell:** Replace commentary with dialogue, behavior, expressions, or actions where possible. But know that for expediency, sometimes you just have to *tell* through narration/exposition. Telling is not wrong.

- **Describe vivid settings:** Readers need a sense of time and place. Painting pictures with words establishes context. Develop scenes. Describe cultures, environments, noises, terrains, structures, and possessions. Establish geography, climate, history, social context, and the time and season of events.

- **Make minor events major:** Take tidbits to a higher level. Make the inconsequential consequential. Embellish with absorbing details and meaning. Mastering this ability provides an opportunity to stand out as a writer.

- **Introduce senses into scenes:** Consider including at least one sensory reaction in every scene.

- **Interject sentiment:** Thread in emotions. Express spiritual connections, passions, and relationships with people, animals, and nature. Give characters a pet. Cultivate relationships. Layer on feelings, while avoiding the words *feel, felt, knew, learned, or thought* (show—don't tell).

- **Relate personal experiences of characters to historical events:** Describing the time, place, and setting in which characters live provides context and color. Include both big-bang and minor past events. Both can have major consequences. Flashbacks can be used if masterfully executed.

- **Evaluate passive voice:** Consider changing passive voice sentences to active ones. Passive voice is *not* wrong, but writing is generally stronger when active voice is used.

- **Manage the "person" factor:** When writing memoir in first person, take out self-indulgent remarks and *I's*, *me's*, and *my's* when possible. When writing in second person for nonfiction/how-to books, take out *you* and *your* when possible while remembering those words are vital. And they bring the writer closer to readers.

- **Interject voice:** Look for ways to express a unique author voice. Build out descriptions of events and scenes in clever, unusual ways. Express yourself freely without intruding on the story. Give the writing personality and delight the reader.

- **Interject humor:** Consider the light side of stories. Apply the stand-up comic technique of carrying a joke throughout a piece or chapter (don't overdo) and use it in the ending. Introduce a quirky, comedic character—a sidekicks to either the protagonist or the villain. Develop colorful minor characters.

- **Assess metaphors, similes, and clichés:** Use original metaphors and similes only and don't overdo. Too many signals amateur and inhibits their effect. Avoid clichés altogether. They are trite. Use your own fabulous words.

- **Tighten up:** Remove unnecessary words and redundant sentences and paragraphs. Don't state the obvious. This is challenging, but it makes all the difference. Stephen King went beyond Faulkner's clichéd *kill your darlings* and said: "Revising a story down to the bare essentials. . .is like murdering children, but it must be done."

- **Avoid empty words:** Avoid *some, any, the, that, even, just,* and *all* where possible. In the case of *it, they, them, this, item, thing,* and *something,* consider substituting more descriptive words. These words are okay to use, but do so judiciously. Reconsider starting a sentence with *there is* or *there are.*

- **Eliminate distracting words:** Evaluate the value of every word. Don't use unnecessary or redundant words. Pay special attention to overuse of adjectives and adverbs. Stronger nouns or verbs often make them unnecessary. Use words like *very, really, rather, somewhat, pretty, virtually, actually, clearly,* and *certainly* sparingly, if at all.

- **Evaluate word selection:** Replace trite words with more interesting, descriptive ones, but don't use a big word when a simple one will do. Make certain words used match the dictionary definition. Select the perfect word. If you can't think of one, put a less than perfect one into a thesaurus and see what comes up. Don't use an important word twice in a sentence or paragraph. Don't use unique, flashy words or phrases (examples: pizzazz, trepidation, potent, celestial) more than two or three times in a book unless they are theme related.

- **Look for words or phrases to emphasize:** Use italics, quotes, or bolding for emphasis in nonfiction. (Don't overdo.) Rarely use these in fiction. They can distract from the story, particularly bolding. Avoid underlining.

- **Improve sentences:** Go over every sentence looking for a way to improve it. Consider structure and its order in the paragraph. Vary sentence structure. Starting every sentence with a noun is boring. The poetry trick of putting important or strong words at the end of lines can improve sentences.

- **Improve paragraphs:** Place the most important sentences at the beginning and ending of paragraphs. The first sentence should be a topical one. Every sentence in a paragraph should support it in some manner. Avoid redundant sentences (two sentences that say the same thing but in a different way). Make the last sentence a clarifying statement, a summarizing point, or a potent snippet. Consider its role in transitioning.

- **Assess adjectives:** Use sparingly and no more than two at a time, except occasionally for effect. Stacking adjectives often happens when the writer didn't find the right noun. Follow punctuation rules when using two adjectives together. A hyphen or comma may be required. When compound adjectives are used before a noun, hyphenate. For example: a well-known speaker. If both adjectives can be used alone with the noun, separate them with a comma. For example: a smart, ambitious businessman.

- **Eliminate adverbs:** Stephen King said, *Adverbs are not your friends. The road to hell is paved with them.* Verbs are usually stronger without them. Choose a stronger verb. Sometimes you've just got to use an adverb, but experts suggest no more than two or three per book is best. If a word ends in *ly*, consider taking it out.

- **Check spelling:** Read out loud word by word or even syllable by syllable. Verify spelling of any questionable words. Don't rely on spellcheck and watch out for auto-correct. If auto-correct changes the word "sentence" to "suntan," both you and your reader will be confused. (It can happen.)

- **Enhance the format:** Introduce white space. Break up long paragraphs. Vary paragraph sizes. For nonfiction, indent whole paragraphs for emphasis, use bullets, and create lists.

- **Check punctuation:** Assure consistent application of rules.

- **Check grammar:** Review for subject/verb agreement, proper and consistent tense and person, and proper sentence structure.

## Reading Run-Throughs

- **Read the manuscript when fresh:** Let it bake. Put it aside for a while and then do another run-through.

- **Read from large print (zoom in):** Mistakes will pop out that would not be noticed in smaller print.

- **Read the manuscript out loud:** This reveals awkward sentence structure. Evaluate the flow.

- **Read the manuscript wearing other hats:** Pretend you are other people while reading, including your harshest critic. Polish the manuscript so it's difficult for that person to challenge anything in it.

- **Read the manuscript for fun:** Pretend you are a member of your audience. Did the tone and content reflect your vision and purpose? Did you enjoy it?

## SWEEPS—FIND AND FIX

The following craft recommendations don't always mean alternatives are wrong, and some rules are controversial among experts. Also, there are reasons to break rules. Writers often violate them in the interest of style and practicality. In general, though, complying with the rules of craft is a gift to readers, and compliance is important to agents, publishers, and contest judges. For this reason, it's best to stay away from controversial craft issues in the first few pages. Wait until you've established your credibility.

It's your call as the writer as to what extent craft is embraced. Don't let its challenges overwhelm and take away the joy of writing. Creation and sharing of a story trumps craft, especially in the case of memoir where it's more important a life story is captured than that it is executed perfectly.

Use the computer "find" capability to search for opportunities for craft improvement. Below are the most common *find and fix* opportunities. It would be a major task to search all of them, and one would have to question your sanity if you did so. However, just reading this list will help you recognize what to watch out for as you polish compositions. Focus on those important to you and those you tend to use improperly. (Note: if any of the following terms or rules are unfamiliar, Google them.)

---

## Review for Possible Deletion or Substitution

Following are words you should avoid *when possible*. **They are not wrong.** Most are in every book or composition, including this one, but they are often overused, unnecessary, or trite. Some are out of favor with writing experts, agents, and publishers because they cry out for better words. Search for them and take them out or rewrite to avoid them where you deem appropriate.

**That, The, Now, Then, Still, Yet, Well, Just, Some, Got, Get, Even, Must, Any, All, Rather, Very**

**Somewhat, Kind Of, Sort Of, Most, A Little, A Lot, Almost, Just About, Pretty, Pretty Much, Quite**

**Might, May, Maybe, Perhaps, Probably** - Sometimes you've just got to use them. Do so judiciously.

**Adverbs:** Use sparingly. Often verbs are stronger on their own. For example: *It was awful* is stronger than *it was truly awful*. Search for words ending in "ly" and reconsider them. Examples: **Practically, Virtually, Literally, Roughly, Fairly, Relatively, Moderately, Slightly, Clearly, Nearly, Truly, Actually, Certainly, Really, Suddenly.**

**Adverb location:** Can be either before or after the verb.

**Never, Always, or Every:** Use only when word is literally true.

**Had, Has, Would, Should, Could:** These suggest tense or strength issues: Use "Dad stoked the fire" not "Dad *would* stoke the fire." If using *had* often, examine the tense in which you write.

**The fact is, as a matter of fact,** or **in order to:** Don't use these.

**It, There, This, They, Thing, Something, Item:** These are *empty* or *dummy words*. Use more descriptive ones where possible. Avoid starting sentences with *There is* or *There are* when possible. Sometimes you just gotta.

**Basically, Totally,** and the vernacular **Like:** Don't use, even in conversation—unless you're at a rave concert in California.

**Like:** When used in simile (analogies), *like* is a good word, but don't overuse. Alternatives to *like* in simile are: *as, as though, as if,* and *similar to.* (Using too many *similes* or *metaphors* weakens their impact and is amateur.)

**Tried to, Started to, Began to:** Get down to what is happening. Use "She cried" instead of "She began to cry." Avoid *tried.* Someone either did something or they didn't. (There are exception to this.)

**Feel, Felt, Seems, Noticed, Looked, Saw, Heard, Knew, Learned, Thought, Realized, Wondered, Guessed, Hoped:** You may be *telling* when *showing* is better. Show through action, behavior, expression, or dialogue.

**Prepositional phrases:** These are okay to use but keep them to a minimum, especially when in compound sentences. Sweep for **of, to, in, by, for** and evaluate for possible rewrite.

**The "ing" words:** Using too many words ending in "ing" is not good craft. Beginning a sentence with an "ing" word is okay occasionally to vary sentence structure, but don't do it too often. Do a sweep for "ing" and reevaluate its use.

**I, My, Me, Myself:** The too frequent use of these words in memoir and other first person writing is distracting. They are important words, but rewrite to eliminate where possible.

# Review for Good Craft

**Person:** First Person: **I, My, Me, We, Us, Our, Ours.** Second Person: **You, Your, Yours.** Third Person: **He, Him, His, She, Her, Hers, They, Them, Their.** Sweep and check for consistency of person. Some shifts in person are appropriate, but execute them expertly so readers aren't jolted.

**Active or Passive Voice:** *Passive voice* is **not wrong,** but *active voice* is stronger. **Passive:** The house was painted by Al. **Active:** Al painted the house. Sweep for passive verbs = **be, by, being, been, was, were, is.** These words suggest *passive voice.* Consider using *active voice.* (Don't let anyone tell you to "avoid using *was.*" Doing so is a way to avoid passive voice, so every *was* is worth assessing, but you can't write in past tense or write a memoir without it.)

**Quotation Marks:** Sweep to assure periods and commas are *always* inside quotation marks. Question marks and exclamation marks can be inside or outside depending on whether they are part of the quote.

**Question Marks:** Search for **Who, What, Why, When, Where, Do** and **How** and check for questions marks. Don't use it if question is rhetorical (requires no response).

**Spacing after a period:** Search for two spaces at the end of sentences. Reduce them to one.

# GRAMMAR/WRITING RULES

These are rules agents, publishers, judges, seasoned writers, and most readers look for when assessing a writer's work. Watch for them when doing revision, editing, run-throughs, and sweeps. Many are too complex to cover in detail here. An Internet search is an efficient way to explore details. Google can be your best friend.

**That, This, Which, and Who rules:**
*That* vs *This* is determined by proximity (Caution: *This* might imply present tense.)

*That* vs *Which* (Clue: *Which* is preceded by a comma.)

*That* vs *Who* - Use *who* when referring to people (not *that*). Use *that* when referring to a company, event, or a thing. There is controversy when it comes to animals. The trend is to use *who* if the animal has a close relationship and has a name. Otherwise, use *it* or *that*. A skunk is most likely *it*.

**Gender rules:** The plurals *them, their,* and *they* are generally accepted now as a way to avoid the singular gender nouns *he* and *she*. However, controversy exists on this point.

**Who vs Whom:** Some consider *whom* too formal. It rarely sounds right since most people don't use it in speech. (Tip: Mentally re-word the sentence. If *him* sounds right, use *whom*. If *he* sounds right, use *who*.) Use *whom* when it's the object of a preposition unless it sounds awkward, which it sometimes does.

**Lay(s), Laid, Laying** = set *object* down.
**Lie(s), Lay(s), Laying, Lain** = a *person* rests or reclines.

**It's vs Its:** *It's* is a contraction for *It is*. *Its* shows possession. This may be the most common error in writing. (Consider replacing *It* with a more descriptive word.)

**If vs Whether:** *If* = conditions / *Whether* = choices

**However vs Nevertheless:** Both show contrast between two sentences. *Nevertheless* is more formal.

**Can vs May:** *Can* = ability / *May* = permission (When speaking, who cares which is used? When writing, it matters.)

**Awhile vs A While:** a*while* = adverb / *a while* = a period of time (Insert "for" in front of *awhile*. If it works, use *a while*.)

**Affect vs Effect:** *Affect* = verb / *Effect* = noun

**i.e. vs e.g.:** *i.e.* = that is / *e.g.* = for example. There is controversy over usage and punctuation on this. An alternative is to use *that is* or *for example* instead of *i.e.* or *e.g.*

**Onto vs On To:** O*nto* = upon / Otherwise use O*n To*

**Into vs In To:** *Into* = preposition expressing motion / *In To* = adverb

**I, My,** and **Me:** These are last when used with another person. (*Mike and I* or *My friends and me*.) *Me* vs *My* is tricky. So is M*yself*. (Google to discover proper usage.)

**You're vs Your:** *You're* is a contraction for *you are*. *Your* shows possession. (Seems everyone should know this, but how many times have you seen it used wrong on Facebook.)

**They're** = they are / **Their** = possession / **There** = place (Consider replacing these with more descriptive words.)

**There is  vs  There are:** The verb *is* or *are* is determined by whether the object of that verb is singular or plural. Examples: *There is one cabin. There are many cabins.* (Rewrite to avoid starting a sentence with these when possible. Never use on the first few pages where you absolutely want to impress.)

**Non words:** Don't use *Anyways, Everywheres, Hisself, Irregardless, Nowheres, Theirselves, Ain't* unless in dialogue where such words reflect a character's lack of refinement.

**Forty and Ninety:** *Fourty* or *Ninty* are misspelled.

**Around** = in the area of  /  **Round** = shape or not exact number  /  **A Round** = Don't use

**Alright** is not a word. Use **All Right**

**All Ready** = fully prepared / **Already** = previously

**Fewer** = number (counted)  /  **Less** = measurement (time, distance, amount)

**Backward(s):** Backward is American, Backwards is English. Same for Afterward/Afterwards. Neither is wrong. Be consistent.

**Off:** Don't say *off of.* Just say *off*—usually.

**Similar words with different meanings:** Such words are often used incorrectly. Watch out for them. An almost infinite number of them exist. Here are a few:

Who's vs Whose / Chose vs Choose / Loose vs Lose / Lead vs Led / Whether vs Weather / Met vs Meant / Bear vs Bare / Breath vs Breathe / Allusion vs Illusion / Aid vs Aide / Accept vs Except / Insure or Assure vs Ensure / Convince vs Persuade. (When questioning which word to use, Google both, for example; *Met vs Meant*. You'll get your answer quickly.)

**"IE" rule:** Not all words follow the rule *i* **before** *e,* **except after** *c,* **or when sounded like** *a*: *weird, being, ancient, foreign, caffeine, either, feisty, height, leisure, protein, science, reimburse, seize, sovereign, species, society, and sufficient.*

**Parallel phrasing:** Phrasing of each item in a series should be compatible. Start each part the same way. Also, use compatible structure in compound sentences when possible. Parallel writing is a complicated process, but doing it properly is the sign of an expert. Google it to learn more.

**But, And, So, Yet, Or:** These coordinating conjunctions usually connect two complete sentences into compound sentences. If each sentence has a noun and a verb, the conjunction is preceded with a comma. If not, don't use a comma. Use compound sentences economically and consider breaking them into separate sentences, especially if phrases are also involved. It's generally accepted now to start a sentence with one of these conjunctions, but don't overdo, and don't do so on the first few pages where you want to establish your awareness of craft.

**Compound vs Complex sentences:** A compound sentence with a prepositional phrase is called a complex sentence. Punctuation can be tricky and there is controversy. Just be consistent. (For example: *Harry hid the gun and, on this occasion, he didn't hide it under the mattress.* Ordinarily, with a compound sentence, the comma would go before the *and*. In this complex one, some authors put it after.)

**Subject/Verb agreement:** If the subject is plural, the verb has no *s*. If the subject is singular, the verb has an *s*. For example: *He runs. They run.* **Note:** *Was* is used with a singular subject (He was); W*ere* with a plural subject (They were)—except when a *condition* is involved (*If* he *were).*

**Dialogue attributions:** Put *he said/she said* **after** the quote (usually). Don't use fancy words in an attribute. Don't use attributes after the first time for each character in a two-way conversation, unless needed for clarification of who's talking. If more than two people are talking, an occasional attribute may be required to clarify who is speaking. Develop characters so the reader knows who's talking by the way they talk, their behavior, or mannerisms.

**Exclamation marks:** Rarely is an *exclamation mark* appropriate. Most experts say to use it *only* to show excessive excitement or shouting. Never use more than one together (!!!). Doing so is amateur squared.

**A series separated by commas:** If possible, put the shortest phrase in a series first and the longest last (perhaps making it a zinger). Use the *Oxford comma* (final comma in a series before the *and* or *or*).

**Commas:** Don't use a comma before *that, because, as, since, or as well.* Use a comma before *such as* and none after when it is followed by an example. Use a comma before *which* and words ending in *ing* (usually). Use a comma after introductory prepositional phrases (not required if just two or three words). Don't use a comma when only the month and year are used (June 2016).

**Periods -** *There's not much to say about the period except that most writers don't reach it soon enough.*—William Zinsser. Use once space after a period at the end of a sentence.

**Hyphen / *en* dash / *em* dash:** Know the difference between these. Use them properly. (Google them.) Don't put a space before or after them.

**Dash:** Avoid using *two hyphens* for a dash. Doing so is not wrong, but it implies "amateur." Use the *em* dash (—). Most computers have a function for generating an *em* dash. The dash is used in place of commas for emphasis, to indicate an interruption, or to suggest "more to come" when used at the end of a sentence. Use no space before or after the *em* dash.

**Ellipses (. . .):** Indicates an omission. Put a space between each period. If used after a complete sentence, a fourth dot is required. It looks like this: My *newborn grandson was smart—above average. . . .*

**Epigraph:** This is a quote after chapter titles and before the text. Be consistent with format, type style, and use of italics or quotation marks. An epigraph also works well as a quote on the blank page across from the Table of Contents. This can hint at the book's theme, convey an important message, and add interest.

# EXAMPLES OF FIRST SENTENCES

Following are examples of first sentences (and possibly more) that create curiosity, establish point of view, identify main characters, incorporate tension or conflict, and hint at the theme:

———————————

Sheridan sobbed in the interview, so Conner hired her, not that the leather skirt and handcuffs hanging from her studded belt had anything to do with his decision.

Travis could never top Dixie. She tossed off verbal hand grenades like they were grapes falling off a counter. He came home from hunting, boasting about bagging a big buck. She used her swollen belly like a howitzer and said, "Yeah, well, I made a kidney."

Gage took what he wanted. Ellie knew later he would take more, and she would have to kill him.

Percy ignored the primal wailing from Wanda as he crammed Max's severed head into the barrel and considered shoving her into it as well.

Mavis got pregnant trying to help Wally quit smoking, and that changed everything.

All three of Cecil's wives died, and no one in Ada knew it—until the Internet happened.

Blake's hellcat girlfriend, Ruby, introduced an emotional terrain that darted around like a laser light and almost got him killed.

The only good news Max had to offer Amanda after the fiasco at their wedding was that at least he didn't get blood on her dress.

After being gone for three years, Gus marched into Mandy's kitchen and checked the cabinet to see if the Jack Daniels was still there.

Newbury, Iowa, was a town marinated in righteous Methodists not open to the invasion of an enthusiastic southern Baptist like Val, a guy hell-bent on saving souls and bedding women.

Colt walked in looking better than any man should, and a brouhaha swirled and rumbled in Brandy's head.

Newt noted that some women got prettier as you got to know them, but Lucy, well, she just ugly-ed up over time.

Jason's mom killed his pet rat with a broom when he was five, and he didn't speak for two years.

Brandy danced naked as the firemen packed up equipment after freeing her toe from the bathtub faucet. Sheriff Hollis sweated.

Jody lay on the bathroom floor after throwing up. Buck hovered in the doorway in his pointy-toed, roach-killer boots and asked if she was going to fix dinner.

Moose rode his motorcycle through a bunch of swarming bees one day, which explained the amputation.

# RECOMMENDED READINGS

## On Writing
William Zinsser - *On Writing Well*
Stephen King - *On Writing*
Anne Lamott - b*ird by bird*
William Bernhardt - *Red SneakerWriting Series:*
  *Sizzling Style, Powerful Premise, Excellent Editing,*
  *Dynamic Dialogue, Creating Character, Perfect Plot,*
  *Story Structure, Thinking Theme, Dazzling Descriptions*
William Kessler - *Story Masters*
Lisa Cron - *Story Genius*
Richard D. Bank - *The Everything Guide to Writing Nonfiction*
Dinty W. Moore - *Crafting the Personal Essay: A Guide to Writing*
  *and Publishing Creative Nonfiction*
Mary Buckham - *Writing Active Settings*
Jack Bickham - *Scene & Structure*
Orson Scott Card - *Characters and Viewpoint*
June Casagrande - *It Was the Best of Sentences, It Was the*
  *Worst of Sentences*
Constance Hale - *Sin and Syntax* (info on voice, show vs tell,
  and syntax—word order)
Marcia Riefer Johnston - *Word Up!*
Vivian Cook - *All in a Word: 100 Delightful Excursions into*
  *the Use and Abuse of Words*
Theodore A. Rees Cheney - *Getting the Words Right*
Francine Prose - *Reading Like a Writer*
Susan Bell - *The Artful Edit*
Sara Gruen - *Water for Elephants* (prologue example)
Ron J. Johnson - *Joe* (how to fill in the blanks example)
David Sedaris - (vignettes, humor, and developing tidbits example)
Brent van Staalduinen - Writers' Blog

## On Memoir
Beth Kephart - *Handling the Truth*
William Zinsser - *Inventing the Truth—The Art and Craft of Memoir*
Mary Carr - *The Art of Memoir*
Melanie Brooks - *Writing Hard Stories*
Roger Rosenblatt - *Unless You Move the Human Heart*
Nikki Hanna - *Capture Life—Write a Memoir*

## Memoirs

Frank McCourt - *Angela's Ashes*
Janet Walls - *The Glass Castle*
Cea Sunrise Person - *North of Normal*
Malcolm Cowley - *The Dream of Golden Mountains*
Jill Ker Conway - *The Road from Coorain*
J. D. Vance - *Hillbilly Elegy*
Amy Tan - *Where the Past Begins: A writer's Memoir*
Joan Didion - *The Year of Magical Thinking* (creative nonfiction)
Azar Nafisi - *Reading Lolita in Tehran* (creative nonfiction)
Nikki Hanna - Red Heels and Smokin'

## On Printing/Publishing

The Alliance of Independent Authors - *Choosing A Self-Publishing Service*
Martha Maeda - *Book Publishing 101*
Marilyn Ross and Sue Collier - *The Complete Guide to Self-Publishing* (encyclopedic)
Sharlene Martin, Anthony Flacco - *Publish Your Nonfiction Book*
Brent Sampson - *Sell Your Book on Amazon*
Chris McMullen - *How to Self-Publish a Book on Amazon.com*
Nikki Hanna - *Listen Up, Writer—How Not to Write Like an Amateur*

Note: Amazon's old printing company, CreateSpace, merged into Amazon's Kindle Direct Publishing (KDP), so some of the information in the above sources will be out of date, unless the authors have updated their books. Those published in late 2018 and forward are more likely to be up to date. (This merger is an example of the dynamic nature of the publishing industry.)

## Reference Guides

*The Chicago Manual of Style* (used by journalists)
Strunk and White - *The Elements of Style* (pocket size)
*Modern Language Association's Standard Format*Susan Thurman - *The Only Grammar Book You'll Ever Need*

# WORKSHOPS AND PRESENTATIONS
By Nikki Hanna

## LISTEN UP, WRITER
How NOT to Write Like an Amateur

**Find Joy and Purpose in Writing:** This session encourages writers to take a fresh look at why they write, to develop a definition of success that taps into innate talents, and to explore options. There is more to writing than selling books, making money, and becoming famous.

**Tap into Craft—The Road to Authorship:** Craft issues can derail even the most talented writers. This session reveals common craft mistakes writers make—the ones that shout amateur.

**Get the Most Out of Revision, Editing, and Proofing:** This session assures a writer is competitive in the writing market—that he produces work that impresses agents, publishers, and judges.

**Nail the Structure—Beginnings, Endings, and In Between:** This session covers how to write compelling beginnings and endings and how to keep the middle of a composition from slumping.

**Write with Voice, Style, and Humor:** This session shows writers how to find their own unique voice and style so their writings stands out from other writers and delights readers through humor.

**Capture Life through Memoir—Writing the Hard Stuff:** This workshop shows how both novice and seasoned writers can write a captivating life story and how to write about difficult times.

**Create Compelling Nonfiction:** This session covers the writing principles that apply to various categories of nonfiction. Writing tips that apply to other genres are also revealed.

**Apply Winning Strategies to Writing Contests:** Participants learn how to be more competitive in contests and how strategically to select contests. What judges look for when comparing entries is explored.

**Evaluate Printing, Publishing, and Marketing Options:** This session discloses nuances of the industry and describes the pros and cons of various publishing strategies.

neqhanna@sbcglobal.net - www.nikkihanna.com

# BOOKS BY NIKKI HANNA
Available on Amazon, Kindle, and ww.nikkihanna.com

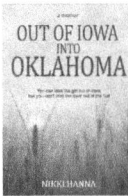

### OUT OF IOWA INTO OKLAHOMA
**You Can Take the Girl Out of Iowa, but You Can't Take the Iowa Out of the Girl**
This saucy and touching memoir about a woman who grew up on an Iowa farm, moved to Oklahoma, and became a successful business executive, chronicles the challenges of adjusting to diverse cultures. Hanna muddles through cultural shifts with grit and moxie.

### CAPTURE LIFE - WRITE A MEMOIR
**Create a Life Story—Leave a Legacy**
Capture Life provides the inspiration and nudge readers need to get started writing life stories. Hanna's humor thoroughly entertains while introducing writing techniques, tedious craft details, and step-by-step instructions on simple and inexpensive ways to print and publish a memoir in book form.

### WRITE WHATEVER THE HELL YOU WANT
**Finding Joy and Purpose in Writing**
Few writers achieve the industry measure of success, which is selling lots of books. Most are frustrated and harboring a sense of failure. Hanna does not suggest writers give up dreams of selling books, but that they explore alternative paths to achievement and re-define success so it is attainable.

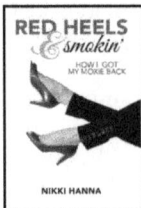

### RED HEELS AND SMOKIN'
**How I Got My Moxie Back**
A playful and inspiring tale of the adventures of a woman who redefined aging, this memoir recounts the transitional years of the author's life after retirement. Readers will root for her rally and be inspired to strategize to achieve one of their own.

## NEAR SEX EXPERIENCES
### A Woman in Crescendo, Aging with Bravado

A playful romp through the process of aging, this collection of vignettes introduces fresh perspectives on the challenges of growing old. Deeply touching stories, thoughtful musings, inspired poetry, and tales laced with wicked wit and lessons-learned entertain and enlighten.

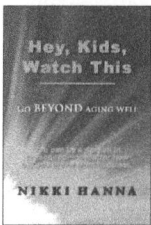

## HEY, KIDS, WATCH THIS
### Go BEYOND Aging Well

An older person can be a person in crescendo—no matter how old they are or what happens. Hanna shows how people create legacy through how they view themselves as older people and how they live their third trimester of life. Readers are encouraged to age in a way that softens the lives of others.

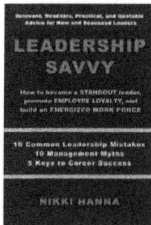

## LEADERSHIP SAVVY
### How to Become a Stand-Out Leader, Promote Employee Loyalty, and Build an Energized Workforce

Fresh, relevant, and practical advice for both novice and experienced leaders is revealed in this candid and perceptive book on leadership. Hanna defines leadership as "service to those you lead." She shares *Ten Common Leadership Mistakes*, *Ten Management Myths*, and *Five Keys to Career Success,* which are potent and novel strategies for setting a leader apart.

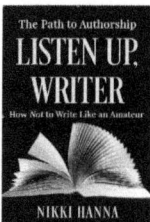

## LISTEN UP, WRITER
### How Not to Write Like an Amateur

Developed as part of a writer education series Hanna presents at writers' conferences and workshops, this book offers strategies designed to achieve *authorship*. It includes advice rich with innovative perspectives that promote exceptional writing results. A blueprint for keeping submissions out of reject piles of agents, publishers, and contest judges, *Listen Up, Writer* is a valuable resource for both novice and seasoned writers.

# ABOUT THE AUTHOR

When asked to describe herself in one sentence, Nikki Hanna said, "I'm a metropolitan gal who never quite reached the level of refinement and sophistication that label implies." The contradictions reflected in this description are the basis of her humorous prose. She has a BS Degree in Business Education and Journalism and an MBA from The University of Tulsa. A retired CPA and Toastmaster, Hanna has years of experience in management and as an executive for one of the country's largest companies. She also served as a consultant on national industry task forces, as a board member for corporations, and as an advisor on curriculum development and strategic planning for educational institutions and charity organizations.

Hanna describes her writing as irreverent, quirky, and laced with humor and strong messages. As an author, writing coach, teacher, and writing contest judge, she is dedicated to inspiring others. She speaks on the craft of writing, memoir writing, and finding joy and purpose in writing as well as on aging, leadership, and women's issues.

In addition to numerous awards for poetry, essays, books, and short stories, Hanna received the Oklahoma Writers' Federation's *Crème de la Crème* Award and the Rose State College Outstanding Writer Award. Book awards include the National Indie Excellence Award, the USA Best Book Finalist Award, two international Book Excellence Awards, four Independent Book Awards, and an IPPY award. Her books are available on Amazon and Kindle and through her website.

Hanna lives in Tulsa, Oklahoma. Her children have decided she has become a bit of a pistol in her old age. Four grandchildren consider her the toy fairy, and those in California believe she lives at the airport.

---

neqhanna@sbcglobal.net
www.nikkihanna.com

www.ingramcontent.com/pod-product-compliance
Lightning Source LLC
Chambersburg PA
CBHW032118040426
42449CB00005B/188